PRAISE FOR
HOPE IN A WORLD GONE MAD

In *Hope in a World Gone Mad*, Gary invites his readers into a conversation on grief, God, and hope. The reader gets to listen in on a conversation, that honestly, we've all wanted to have regarding grief. So, grab a cup of coffee and listen in.
—Dr. Troy Allen, Senior Pastor,
First Baptist Church, College Station

Hope in a World Gone Mad is a different sort of book. Written as a personal conversation, Gary digs into the tough situation that grievers experience today - handling their own painful losses while dealing with an upside-down, fearful world. We need help and hope, and this book contains a lot of both.
—Dr. Charles W. Page, MD, author of
A Spoonful of Courage for the Sick and Suffering

Gary Roe's new book, *Hope in a World Gone Mad*, helps us process through how we deal with loss in a broken world where things just seem to get worse. Presented in a conversational style, Gary walks a grieving individual through the realities of their pain, hurt, and confusion to a place of real hope and comfort. The chapters of this book are written in bite-sized pieces so a person can immerse themselves in this conversation as little or as much as that person desires. Gary has provided a clear path from hurt to hope for a person working through any type of loss. Anyone who reads Gary's book will appreciate the tenderness with which Gary moves us from despair to hope, from pain to peace, and from confusion to comfort. I highly recommend this book for the hurting and for those walking with others through the pain of loss.

—Reggie Coe, Pastor and Chaplain,
Grace Church, Wichita Falls, Texas

If you, like me and so many others, are experiencing profound grief over the loss of a loved one, the last thing you need is the added burden of living in a world that has gone completely insane. In this latest work, Gary Roe approaches this subject in true Christian love. In a warm one-to-one conversation, Gary gently leads the reader to an understanding of God's amazing love for us, and the salvation He provides through the sacrifice of Jesus Christ. Exactly what a fearful and grieving heart needs. Once you start reading this book you cannot put it down.

—Dennis Baer, survivor of multiple close losses

Gary Roe's new book, *Hope in a World Gone Mad*, is a short read that I believe everyone who is walking the road of grief should read. This book is different from other books written by Gary in that instead of just giving the reader human wisdom and grief skills (which he does) Gary comes right to the point in showing the reader who their source is and where true peace in a time of loss comes from. As a Christian Pastor, I was delighted to read a book from an expert in the field of grief who shares some of the things I share with my church grief groups. I would highly recommend *Hope in a World Gone*

Mad, I intend to see that Grief Groups I resource and lead will have a copy available for each participant.

—Rev. Louie Lyon, Pastoral Care Pastor,
Dove of the Desert United Methodist Church,
Glendale, Arizona

Hope In a World Gone Mad is a conversational book, personally and beautifully written. Gary explores and examines the world of grief and loss in a world of fear and uncertainty. He brings us hope, help, and healing, something that we all need now. And my hope is that everyone who reads this book receives as much comfort and reassurance as I have received through Gary and his thoughtful, insightful, and encouraging words.

—Joan Pruitt, Licensed Professional
Counselor, Hospice of Wichita Falls

When I lost my husband, I questioned God and almost Him pushed away. This sensitive book helped me realize that Jesus walked with me every step (and even carried me). It is written differently in that it is almost a counseling conversation, which helped me to relate even more to my need!

—Sue Beabout, bereaved spouse

I have read *Hope in a World Gone Mad* and recommend it without hesitation. I believe the crux of Gary Roe's latest book is this: "The world is full of noise and distraction. All that matters is Jesus and keeping my eyes on Him." World chaos coupled with personal grief is extraordinarily difficult, but this book can help calm your mind and strengthen your faith.

—Nancy Breedlove, retired educator
& perpetual student of life

HOPE
IN A WORLD GONE MAD

FINDING GOD IN GRIEF, FEAR, & UNCERTAINTY

GARY ROE

Hope in a World Gone Mad:
Finding God in Grief, Fear, and Uncertainty
Copyright © 2021 by Gary Roe
All rights reserved.
First Edition: 2021

Print ISBN: 978-1-950382-57-6
KDP Print ISBN: 978-1-950382-56-9
eBook ISBN: 978-1-950382-55-2

Cover and Formatting: Streetlight Graphics

Published by: Healing Resources Publishing All Bible references are from THE HOLY BIBLE, NEW INTERNATIONAL VERSION®, NIV® Copyright © 1973, 1978, 1984, 2011 by Biblica, Inc.® Used by permission. All rights reserved worldwide.

The author is not engaged in rendering medical or psychological services, and this book is not intended as a guide to diagnose or treat medical or psychological problems. If you require medical, psychological, or other expert assistance, please seek the services of your own physician or mental health professional.

No part of this book may be reproduced, scanned, or distributed in any printed or electronic form without permission. Please do not participate in or encourage piracy of copyrighted materials in violation of the author's rights. Thank you for respecting the hard work of this author.

OTHER BOOKS BY GARY ROE

THE COMFORT SERIES

Comfort for Grieving Hearts: Hope and Encouragement in Times of Loss

Comfort for the Grieving Spouse's Heart: Hope and Healing After Losing Your Partner

Comfort for the Grieving Adult Child's Heart: Hope and Healing After Losing Your Parent

Comfort for the Grieving Parent's Heart: Hope and Healing After Losing Your Child

THE GOD AND GRIEF SERIES

Grief Walk: Experiencing God After the Loss of a Loved One

Widowed Walk: Experiencing God After the Loss of a Spouse

THE GOOD GRIEF SERIES

The Grief Guidebook: Common Questions, Compassionate Answers, Practical Suggestions

Grieving the Write Way Journal and Workbook

Aftermath: Picking Up the Pieces After a Suicide

Shattered: Surviving the Loss of a Child

Teen Grief: Caring for the Grieving Teenage Heart

Please Be Patient, I'm Grieving: How to Care for and Support the Grieving Heart

Heartbroken: Healing from the Loss of a Spouse

Surviving the Holidays Without You: Navigating Loss During Special Seasons

THE DIFFERENCE MAKER SERIES

Difference Maker: Overcoming Adversity and Turning Pain into Purpose, Every Day (Adult & Teen Editions)

Living on the Edge: How to Fight and Win the Battle for Your Mind and Heart (Adult & Teen Editions)

TABLE OF CONTENTS

Grief in a World Gone Crazy xvii

1: How Could This Happen? 1

2: I Don't Want It to be True 3

3: Is the Old Normal Gone? 5

4: I Feel Invisible and Alone 7

5: Everything is Shaking 9

6: I Don't Feel Safe Anymore 11

7: I Feel So Confused 13

8: Something Confusing is Going On 15

9: I Thought I Was the Problem 17

10: Nothing Seems to Make Sense 19

11: I Wonder Who I Really Am 21

12: Life Feels Like a War 23

13: I Want to be Seen and Loved 25

14: Created in the Image of God 27

15: Unique in Human History 29
16: The Heart Knows Things the Mind Does Not 31
17: Hearing the Voice of the Heart 33
18: Wanted, Planned, and Personally Created 35
19: There is No Fear in Perfect Love 37
20: I Feel Lighter Somehow 39
21: My Heart is More Relaxed 41
22: Brokenhearted and Crushed 43
23: Stuck in a Cycle 45
24: Coping but Not Going Anywhere 47
25: There Must Be a Better Way 49
26: What If the Answer to Our Problem is a Person? 51
27: When Fear and Anxiety Strike 53
28: I Want to Feel Safe 55
29: I'm So Embarrassed 57
30: We Have a Big Problem 59
31: What Exactly Are We Chasing? 61
32: Looking for Meaning and Worth 63
33: Our Heart Problem 65
34: Trying to Do Life Without God 67
35: The Ultimate Solution 69

36: What If? 71

37: Peaceful, Accepted, and Free 73

38: A Change in Identity 75

39: A Continual Conversation 77

40: A Completely Secure Future 79

41: Religion Verses Relationship 81

42: The Treadmill of Performance 83

43: Walking Through the Fire 85

44: Light in the Darkness 87

45: Not a Way Out but a Way Through 89

46: Fear and Division 91

47: Walking in the Light 93

48: A New Life and a New Home 96

49: On Assignment Away from Home 99

50: An Eternal Mindset 102

51: Running the Race 104

52: Dodging Distractions 106

53: Facing Opposition 108

54: Relentless Love 110

55: Focusing on the Goal 112

56: Trouble Will Come 114

57: Meeting Challenges Head On 116

58: Problems are Opportunities 118

59: Pain Feels Different When
Walking in the Light ... 121

60: Feeling Out of Place ... 123

Gary's Story ... 127

Some Bible Verses Dealing with Fear ... 133

Some Bible Verses Dealing with Anxiety ... 137

Some Bible Verses Dealing with Grief ... 139

Some Bible Verses about Jesus as God ... 143

Additional Resources ... 151

Free Resources ... 153

About the Author ... 155

Acknowledgements ... 157

An Urgent Request ... 159

There is no fear in love.
But perfect love drives out fear.
(1 John 4:18)

Thank you for purchasing *Hope in a World Gone Mad: Finding God in Grief, Fear, and Uncertainty*

No matter what you're going through at present, we hope that you are comforted and encouraged by the pages ahead.

As a thanks, Gary has prepared a free download (PDF) for you.

Download your free PDF today:
"What in the World is Going On?"
https://www.garyroe.com/what-in-the-world

GRIEF IN A WORLD GONE CRAZY

Are you scared, anxious, and grieving?

Chances are you're dealing with a deep, personal loss of some kind. Perhaps several.

On top of that, we live in a world gone crazy. Everything is upside down. Things seem unpredictable, uncertain, and unsafe.

We're battling our own fear and anxiety, while immersed in a world of confusion, panic, and terror. We're grieving and living in a world of grief.

WHO AM I?

Hi. My name is Gary. I serve as an author, speaker, and grief specialist.

You can find my story at the end of this book. For now, I'll just say that my life has been a war.

In childhood, I experienced sexual abuse, emotional abuse, bullying, isolation, and the deaths of family members and friends. My mom slipped away into mental illness, had several breakdowns, and attempted suicide. My dad died suddenly in front of me. All this occurred by the time I was 15.

As a teen, I made a choice to heal and grow through loss and pain. That eventually led to an adult life of helping other hurting, grieving people heal and grow.

Life didn't get any easier in adulthood. The losses kept coming, piling up over the years. Some of them were debilitating.

Yet, I'm tremendously grateful for the healing and growth I've experienced along the way. I'm living proof that anyone can recover, adjust, and learn to use pain for good.

The most important thing about me is that I am a follower of Jesus Christ. He is my life and my hope. Apart from Him, I can do nothing.

Since one of my goals is to write from my heart to yours, my faith is going to be all over these pages. If you're of a different faith or claim no faith at all, I hope you'll stick with me and open your heart to the conversation that follows.

We're all human. We all hurt. We all have hearts that can be broken. We all have longings that cry out from deep within us.

Stay with it. Read to the end. Stay open. See what you think.

I write from personal and professional experience. My vocational mix of grief specialist, theologian, and former missionary, pastor, and hospice chaplain all come into play. I hope you find the following pages comforting, encouraging, and healing.

Most of all, I pray that you will come out of this book with sure and certain hope.

A CONVERSATION OF GRIEF AND HOPE.

This book is written as a conversation. This is not the verbatim record of an actual interaction, but rather an adaptation of numerous conversations I've had with many grieving hearts.

Though every loss and grief process are individual and unique, there are some common patterns that we all experience. Battling fear, anxiety, and uncertainty in grief is something everyone encounters. There are times when we all struggle to find hope.

Our conversation in this book doesn't delve into the intricacies of the grief process. The grief journey is arduous, frustrating, confusing, angering, and packed full of sadness, guilt, regret, and depression. A book could easily be written about each thing in this list.

In this book, we move quickly to the root of all the thoughts and emotions we struggle with. These things come from inside us - from our hearts.

When I use the word *heart*, I'm referring to what the Bible means by *heart*. It includes both our soul and our spirit. Our soul encompasses our minds, our emotions, and our will. Our spirit is the deepest part of us, the essence of who we are.

So, if you're looking for an in-depth analysis of the grief process, this book isn't it. This book is about discovering hope - real hope, lasting hope, eternal hope - amid terrible grief in a world gone mad.

This book is not some magic pill or quick fix. Everyday life is a war, with no immediate end in sight. Each day we wake up to a fierce battle raging in our own hearts and in the world around us.

The real battle is for our hearts.

Jesus said, "In this world you will have trouble. Take heart; I have overcome the world."

We were born into trouble. We will face trouble today. Life is not about getting our way or making things easier somehow. Life is about overcoming.

Let the conversation of hope begin.

1
HOW COULD THIS HAPPEN?

I can't believe my loved one is gone.
How could this happen?
I have no words for this.
I can't even describe the pain.
My heart is in pieces.

Losing a loved one can be one of the most devastating things a person can experience.

Your life has changed forever. Your heart knows this.

I'm so sorry.

Everything seems empty now.
I'm in a daze. I'm stunned.
I don't know how to feel or what to do.
Then I come to my senses and look at the world around me.
What a mess.
What is going on?

Your loss is more than enough to deal with. Yet, your personal world is upside down and at the same time our larger world seems to be falling apart.

Everything is changing so rapidly. Things seem crazy and chaotic. The anger level out there is disturbing.

I can imagine that, on top of your own loss, this feels overwhelming.

It's terrifying.

I'm scared and anxious all the time.

I shake inside.

Sometimes my hands tremble.

That's understandable. I'm scared too.

Fear and anxiety are common in grief, but this situation is unprecedented.

It's like we wake up to a war each day, and we're caught in the middle of it.

It almost seems like we live on a different planet now.

Perhaps we do.

2
I DON'T WANT IT TO BE TRUE

We live in a different world now. You sense this. This greatly adds to and complicates what's happening inside you about your own personal loss.

Let's separate those two for a moment - your personal loss and all the change out in the world.

When you focus on your own loss, what feelings are rustling around in your heart?

> *Shock. I still can't believe it sometimes.*
>
> *I don't want it to be true.*
>
> *Sadness. It's all so sad.*
>
> *I never knew I could be this sad.*

Take your time.
Breathe.

> *I've been angry too. Mad at myself. Mad at the world. Mad at people. Mad at God.*
>
> *I'm frustrated. I'm irritable and impatient.*

> *It's like everything I don't like about myself is leaking out all over everything.*
>
> *I've also felt confused. I can't make sense of it. I can't put it together in my brain.*

I hear you. Keep going.
What else has been happening inside you?

> *Fear. I'm afraid, on some level, all the time.*
>
> *I'm afraid for myself. I'm afraid for the people I love. It's like I'm waiting for another disaster to strike.*
>
> *I'm anxious. I'm anxious about almost everything all the time.*
>
> *I feel like I'm in danger. I'm always scanning for threats of more pain and loss.*
>
> *And I feel guilty - terribly guilty.*
>
> *There are so many things I wish I had said and done. And oh, there are so, so many things I wish I had not said and done.*
>
> *I have so many regrets.*
>
> *I wish I could have a do-over.*

3
IS THE OLD NORMAL GONE?

And, honestly, I'm depressed. Or at least I feel depressed.

I wonder about the meaning of all this. I wonder why I'm here.

I wonder about a lot of things now.

Thank you for sharing with me.

If it helps any, everything you just said is perfectly consistent with the loss you're experiencing.

In other words, these feelings and thoughts are extremely common in grief.

Do you ever feel alone in all this?

Oh gosh, yes.

People I counted on have disappeared. My friends don't contact me.

Those closest to me don't get it.

Everyone looks at me differently, like they're terrified of what I might say or do.

I've even had the thought that people are avoiding me.

Sometimes I feel like I have an infectious disease.

I have felt similar things after my losses. Most people are compassionate for about a month, and then they expect you to be back to normal.

In other words, they expect you to go back to who you were before. But you know that's impossible.

Your loss has changed your world. You are not the same. You will never be the same.

I've never thought of it quite that way.

Yes, I know this.

My world is different. The world itself is changing.

Is the old normal gone?

I don't want to believe that, but I know it's true.

4
I FEEL INVISIBLE AND ALONE

Yes, the old normal is gone. You are different now.

Because you are different, your relationships will be different. Something has happened to you that has not happened to others around you.

This, in and of itself, can cause distance.

> *I can see that. It's like the space between me and some of the people I counted on is widening.*
>
> *People are disappearing on me, right and left. Some have completely evaporated. Poof!*
>
> *I get angry about this.*
>
> *Why are they doing this? Where did they go?*
>
> *I wonder if I ever really knew them.*

That hurts, doesn't it?

Life is hard enough without feeling rejected and abandoned by the people we know and love.

> *Yes, that's it. That's how I feel.*

Rejected. Abandoned. Invisible.

I feel invisible.

I feel alone.

We need each other, especially in times of pain, loss, and uncertainty.

When people walk away from us at such times, it's doubly disturbing and hurtful.

Sadly, many people don't want to understand our grief. Many people can't understand it.

It would be nice if they were at least compassionate and supportive, but that requires an intentional effort on their part to enter our pain.

And most people flee from pain like the plague.

Yes. No wonder I feel alone.

And yet, I know I'm not alone.

You get it. And there are others who get it, right?

5
EVERYTHING IS SHAKING

Yes, there are others who understand. There are compassionate and supportive people out there.

Though you are unique, and your loss is unique, there are others who can walk with you through this.

The road of loss and grief is lonely, but there are many people walking this road.

Yes, you will feel lonely.

But no, you are not alone.

> *Somehow, I know this is true. It must be true.*
>
> *I know everyone is stressed. I know everyone, on some level, is probably anxious and scared too.*
>
> *Maybe people are just overloaded and can't handle any more grief.*
>
> *Even so, you would think those closest to me would be more compassionate.*
>
> *I hope I would be supportive of them, even with all this other chaos going on.*

You know loss, pain, and grief on a deeper level now.

You see it and feel it in your own heart.

You see it and feel it out in the world.

I would think it probably feels like you're surrounded by grief and pain all the time.

> *That's exactly what it feels like.*
>
> *I have my own grief, pain, fear, and anxiety, and then everywhere I go I bump into more.*
>
> *I turn on the TV, and there it is again.*
>
> *I look at my phone, and there's more pain and fear there too.*
>
> *It's all over the media - anger, fear, uncertainty, and hatred.*
>
> *I feel like everything is shaking.*

Perhaps you feel that way because everything *is* shaking.

Maybe you're sensing and feeling reality.

6
I DON'T FEEL SAFE ANYMORE

Yes. Everything is shaking.
That's terrifying.
I feel paralyzed.
I don't know what to do.
I don't know how to do life anymore.
It's like my heart is immobilized.

Look at all that is happening inside you. Look at all that is happening in the world.

No wonder you feel paralyzed.

No wonder you feel anxious. No wonder you're afraid.

Breathe deeply for a moment.

Sometimes we can forget to breathe.

My heart hurts.
It feels like my life as I knew it is over.
I can barely sleep, and when I do, I wake up feeling panicked.

How do I handle this?

Fear, terror, anxiety, and panic are everywhere. Something huge is happening. We can feel tiny and insignificant in the midst of it all.

Fear and anxiety are threatening to take over.

The first key is to know that fear and anxiety are to be expected when you're grieving.

After a loss, your heart shifts more easily into fight-or-flight mode. In fact, your heart can get stuck there at times.

Tiny. That's how I feel.

Like I'm bobbing around in the ocean with no land in sight. I'm just trying to stay afloat.

I don't feel safe anymore.

Anything could happen at any time to anyone.

That's terrifying.

It's hard to feel safe when everything is topsy-turvy and upside down.

The world has changed. We knew what life was, but we don't know what life will be like today or down the road.

Yet, we want to know. That way we can feel like we have a sense of control.

But, of course, control is an illusion. And that's a tough pill to swallow.

7
I FEEL SO CONFUSED

I normally think of myself as strong and independent.
I'm embarrassed.
I'm frightened. Terribly frightened.
I wish I didn't feel this way.
I feel stupid and weak.

Some people feel bad for being scared. Some people see anxiety as a weakness.

Almost everyone sees fear and anxiety as negative and to be avoided at all costs.

After all, who wants to be scared and anxious?

In all this turmoil, I find myself thinking about God.
Is He there? Is He real? Where is He?
If He exists, how does He fit into all this?

Excellent questions.

To help me understand better, can you tell me a little about what you mean by *God*?

I don't want to assume anything. And I want to make sure I meet you where you are, as much as possible.

> *Well, I have this idea that, if God exists, that He is - well, you know - greater than us.*
>
> *He would be more intelligent, more powerful, and, well, more everything.*

What other words would you use to describe your concept of God?

> *I would hope God would be kind. I hope God would be merciful and loving.*
>
> *Honestly, I don't know.*
>
> *I look at the world out there and I see so much beauty and order in creation. I think that whoever or whatever is behind all that must be amazing.*
>
> *And then I look at human beings and all the trouble in the world and wonder if maybe God created everything and then just disappeared.*
>
> *I don't know. I feel so confused about this.*

8
SOMETHING CONFUSING IS GOING ON

You see order, beauty, and goodness out there in nature and naturally think that there's something or someone orderly, beautiful, and good behind all that.

But you look at humanity and wonder whether it's possible that God created the universe and then left it - perhaps even abandoned it.

And you feel confused about all this.

Have I got that right?

Yes.

Do you feel confused often lately?

Yes, I certainly do.

Honestly, I almost feel disoriented - like I'm living in some alternate universe.

Every day I seem to wake up in a world that feels less and less familiar.

Confused and disoriented.

When you're confused, it's because something confusing is going on.

When you feel disoriented, it's because something disorienting is happening around you.

Has your grief journey been confusing at times, even disorienting?

What about the world? Does it seem confusing and disorienting out there right now?

Yes, and yes!

So, I feel confused and disoriented because things are confusing and disorienting.

How obvious is that? Wow.

The confusion is not coming from me - it's coming from outside me.

Is that what you're saying?

9
I THOUGHT I WAS THE PROBLEM

Yes.

If that's true, that the confusion you feel is coming from outside you, do you think that might also be true for the fear and anxiety you're experiencing?

> *Do you mean that when I'm fearful or anxious, it might be because of what's happening around me?*

Yes. Is it possible that when you feel fearful, it's because something fear-producing is going on?

And when you feel anxious, could it be that something anxiety-producing is happening?

> *I want to say, "Well, duh, yeah!"*
>
> *And yet, I've somehow never thought of it that way.*
>
> *I've always thought it was just me.*
>
> *I thought I was the problem.*

We naturally react to what happens to us and around us.

We all have a grid through which we see life. We react and respond according to that grid.

If you perceive something as dangerous, then feeling fearful or anxious would be natural. Fear and anxiety are natural reflexes. They're automatic. You can't stop them.

I'm not sure I understand.

Here's what I mean.

Something unpleasant or disturbing happens. Your natural fight-or-flight mechanism is triggered. This is automatic. It's a reflex.

After your fight-or-flight switch gets flipped, fear and anxiety instantly power to the surface. If the trigger is strong enough, fear can hijack your entire system.

Everyone experiences this. Everyone. Some just hide it better than others. I experience it all the time.

Your fight-or-flight mechanism is built into you for your safety, but it is not designed to be a way of life. That means we must find ways to manage and deal with it, even in a world gone bonkers.

10
NOTHING SEEMS TO MAKE SENSE

Bonkers. I haven't heard that word in a while.
Silly word. Makes me laugh.
I get it.
What I'm feeling is normal for what I'm experiencing.
But now what do I do with it?
I don't want to be terrified and panicked all the time.

No, of course not. And you don't have to be.

Fear is a powerful motivator. Fear is also a terrible motivator. It can cause us to do things that we would normally never do.

Continual fear leads to paranoia. When we live in a state of fear, we can become irrational.

Look at the world out there. Do you see anything irrational going on?

It's hard to not feel fearful when you're surrounded by craziness.

Yes, I can see that.

> *I feel like I've been irrational at times, and I can surely see that in the world right now.*
>
> *Nothing seems to make sense. Everything seems irrational out there.*

And that's terribly disturbing, confusing, and fear-producing.

For you personally, your heart has been hit. When that happens, fear and anxiety will naturally spill out.

Your heart gets bombarded all day, every day. Your heart is getting pummeled right now.

Dealing with all this in a healthy way begins with being kind to yourself.

If you were listening to someone else going through what you're going through, you would be kind to them, right?

> *Of course.*
>
> *I tend to be hard on myself.*
>
> *I have high expectations, even with all that's happening with me and in the world.*
>
> *Pretty ridiculous, huh?*

11
I WONDER WHO I REALLY AM

I don't think it's ridiculous that you're hard on yourself. It's not helpful, but it's not ridiculous.

Many of us are hard on ourselves. I know I am.

Instead of ridiculous, maybe we could say you might not be taking your own heart seriously enough?

Maybe. I don't know.

Sometimes I don't think I know myself or my heart very well.

It's like the real me is in here somewhere but buried under a lot of junk.

I wonder sometimes who I really am and why I'm here.

Speaking of that, can we go back to God again? My mind keeps going back there.

Certainly. What's on your mind?

That's just it. I don't exactly know what's on my mind.

I know that you believe in God. Could you tell me what you think about Him?

I would be glad to share with you what I believe about God.

Would you be okay with me sharing my faith in the context of what you're currently experiencing?

In other words, I don't want to make this about me. I want it to be about you.

Sure. I'm okay with that.

Thank you.

12
LIFE FEELS LIKE A WAR

You just mentioned that you felt like you didn't know yourself or your own heart.

Over 3000 years ago, wise King Solomon said, "Above all else, guard your heart, for it is the spring from which everything else in your life flows."

"Above all else," he said. That means guarding your heart is *the* priority.

That word "guard" is a military term. You're in a war. The world is not kind to your heart. You must guard it.

Your heart is the core of your being. Your heart is who you are.

> *That makes sense.*
>
> *I have always known that there is a deeper part of me down inside somewhere.*
>
> *And this life certainly does feel like a war.*
>
> *How do I guard my heart?*

Let's begin with this.

What are some influences that you sense are dangerous for your heart?

In other words, what's *not* helpful for you right now?

Critical, judgmental people.

Negative, depressing news.

Too much alone time.

Bad personal habits. You know, addictive behaviors.

Do these people or influences also seem to increase your fear and anxiety levels?

Yes!

Okay. So, there's going to be a connection between guarding your heart and your fear and anxiety level.

Now, see if you can name some things that would be helpful to you in this season.

13
I WANT TO BE SEEN AND LOVED

Hmm. Thinking of things that are helpful to me right now is a little tougher.

What we're doing here is helpful - talking about things with someone I trust.

I guess I need support.

I need people who understand - who get it.

It would be helpful if people would let me talk, and if they actually listened.

I know I need to take care of myself, but I'm just so scared and exhausted.

I'm in survival mode.

To guard your heart, you will need to limit your exposure to negative influences and even people who are not helpful to you.

You'll also need to pursue people and influences that *are* healthy and helpful.

What do you think about that?

That makes sense.

I think you know that this is all about people and relationships.

People will make all the difference in your life, one way or another.

If you look deep inside, what do you sense your heart is most longing for?

To be embraced and loved.

To be seen and understood.

To be protected and safe.

Would you say that's probably true for most people?

Yes, I would.

14
CREATED IN THE IMAGE OF GOD

I agree. I believe everyone on the planet longs to be seen, heard, understood, and safe.

All these things we long for are relational. We long for great, even perfect relationships.

Now, here's where my faith in God comes in. See if you can make this leap with me.

What if there was someone who could love you perfectly, knew you completely, and was available all the time?

> *I would say that's amazing, but impossible - at least impossible for another human being.*
>
> *But perhaps not impossible for God?*

Perhaps not impossible for God. But how would we know?

That's where the Bible comes in.

I believe that the Bible is God's Word to us. I believe He has spoken to us and told us who He is, who we are, why we're here, and why the world is the way it is.

> *What does the Bible say about me?*

First of all, the Bible says you are created in the image of God.

Now, that means a lot of things, but let's focus on just a few.

It means that you were not an accident. You were wanted, planned, and personally created by God Himself.

It also means that you were designed for relationships, first with God Himself, and then with other people.

Let's just assume that's true. Does that make sense to you?

Yes, I think so.

15
UNIQUE IN HUMAN HISTORY

BY THE WAY, THIS IS why losing someone special hurts so desperately.

I'm not sure I follow.
Can you explain what you mean?

You are unique in human history. There's never been another person exactly like you, even if you're a twin.

The same was true about your loved one. They were created in the image of God and unique in human history. There will never be another person exactly like your loved one.

Two people, both unique in human history. That means your relationship was also unique. There's never been another relationship exactly like it.

How special is that?

No wonder it hurts. No wonder loss is heartbreaking, even crushing.

I completely get that.
That makes total sense.

No wonder I feel this way.

Now, look deep inside again and feel those longings in your heart - to be completely known, seen, heard, loved, and safe.

Can another human being ever fully, completely meet those longings?

No, I don't think so.

What if God created you with those longings so that you would discover them and begin to seek Him?

In other words, what if God and God alone can fulfill your deepest yearnings?

I guess that's possible.

16
THE HEART KNOWS THINGS THE MIND DOES NOT

If God knows you perfectly, would that also mean He understands the fear, anxiety, and grief that you're experiencing?

What do you think?

> *If God knows everything in my heart, then yes, He would understand what I'm feeling and thinking.*

Take a deep breath. Breathe in through your nose, then out through your mouth.

Good.

Again.

I believe God knows you. I believe He knows everything - I mean everything - about you.

I believe He knows your grief, anxiety, and fear.

I believe He loves you.

> *Okay.*
>
> *That sure sounds good.*

I think there are times when we understand some things with our hearts, even while our minds are still struggling to make sense of it.

What do you think about that?

Absolutely.

I've experienced that many times.

My mind was still questioning, but my heart just "knew."

Would you be open to saying out loud some things I believe to be true about God?

The goal would be to see how your heart responds to these things.

17
HEARING THE VOICE OF THE HEART

I think I get it.

We're not bypassing my mind. We're focusing on my heart.

Yes.

Your mind is always operating.

We're trying to hear the voice of your heart.

I'm okay with that.

My brain has gone around and around over all this stuff anyway with seemingly no progress.

Okay. Feel free to close your eyes or keep them open - whatever feels most comfortable to you.

Now, breathe deeply and slowly - in through your nose, and now out through your mouth.

Again.

One more time.

Now, try repeating after me.

God knows me.

God knows me.

God knows everything about me.

God knows everything about me.

God knows my sorrow, my fear, and my anxiety.

God knows my sorrow, my fear, and my anxiety.

God loves me.

God loves me.

Breathe, slowly and deeply, in through your nose and out through your mouth.
Good.
Again.
One more time.

18
WANTED, PLANNED, AND PERSONALLY CREATED

What happened inside you when you said those things?

I don't know how to describe it.

I guess I could say that it felt good.

I felt peaceful.

I also found myself holding back tears, like something deep inside me was being released.

The Bible tells us that God knows everything. Therefore, He knows you completely, including your deepest longings, fears, and worries.

God tells us that He is indeed your Creator and that He wanted you, planned you, and personally made you in your mother's womb.

If that's true, would it be safe to assume that God knows you better than anyone else, better than even you know yourself?

If God planned and made me, then yes.

Would it make sense that God your Creator knows your true identity, who you are and why you're here?

Yes, that would make sense.

Would it also be reasonable to assume that God is concerned about you, and that He has some guidance about things like fear, anxiety, worry, and grief?

Yes, that seems reasonable.

Okay. I'm going to read a few Bible verses.

As you listen, pay attention to what's happening inside you - in your heart.

I'll read one short passage at a time.

Feel free to close your eyes, if you wish.

19
THERE IS NO FEAR IN PERFECT LOVE

Here we go.

"There is no fear in love. But perfect love drives out fear."

(Pause)

Breathe. Pay attention to what's happening inside you.

(Pause)

"There is no fear in love. But perfect love drives out fear."

That sounds so good.

What is it that sounds good?

I can see that there would be no fear in perfect love.
If I was perfectly loved, why would I ever need to be afraid?
Perfect love sounds wonderful. It sounds safe.

It does sound wonderful and safe.
Let's go to another Bible verse. This is a short one.

This one might bring up a lot of questions. Try to pay attention to what happens in your heart when you hear it.

(Pause)

"God is love."

(Pause)

Keep breathing slowly and deeply.

(Pause)

"God is love."

Wait.

I want to think about that a little more.

(Pause)

Okay. I'm ready.

20
I FEEL LIGHTER SOMEHOW

Here's the next one.

"The Lord is with me; I will not be afraid."

(Pause)

Let me say that again.

"The Lord is with me; I will not be afraid."

Give me just a moment.

(Pause)

Okay.

Good. Keep breathing deeply and slowly.

(Pause)

Here's the next Bible verse. Again, pay attention to what happens in your heart.

"Cast all your anxiety on God, because He cares for you."

(Pause)

Let me say it again.

"Cast all your anxiety on God because He cares for you."

I can feel my body relaxing.
I feel lighter somehow, like something has been released.

Good.
Keep breathing deeply.
One more verse.
Here we go.

21
MY HEART IS MORE RELAXED

THIS IS JESUS SPEAKING.

"My peace I give you. I do not give to you as the world gives. Do not let your hearts be troubled and do not be afraid."

(Pause)

I'll say it again.

"My peace I give you. I do not give to you as the world gives. Do not let your hearts be troubled and do not be afraid."

Peace. I feel peace.

My heart is much more relaxed, calm.

Good. Go ahead and open your eyes.

Thanks for doing that exercise.

If you found that helpful, I'll give you a copy of those Bible verses, and a few others. You can do the same thing on your own.

That would be great.

It's amazing how much more peaceful I feel.

Thanks for that exercise.

If He is really God, then He is omnipresent. He's everywhere all at once. He is always with you. He is here with us, right now.

In the fear, the anxiety, and the grief, God is with you.

I believe He can feel what you feel. He feels your fear, your anxiety, and your grief. If He is God, then He can do that.

22
BROKENHEARTED AND CRUSHED

That makes sense. I've never thought of that before.
I must have thought that God was more, well,
"up there". That He was more impersonal.

He is holy, righteous, and perfect, yes. But He is also more personal than we can imagine.

I believe He is the best possible companion you can have on this painful, exhausting journey.

If He made you, He knows you. If He is God, then He is the only One who knows exactly who you are.

Getting to know Him can be the greatest adventure and comfort in life.

Here's another verse for you:

> "The Lord is close to the brokenhearted. He saves those who are crushed in spirit."

I like that one. I like it a lot.
I've certainly felt brokenhearted and crushed.

I like it too. God is close. Closer than we can fathom.

What we've done is to go to the root of your fears. We've gone to your soul, to your heart.

Many times, we try to deal with fear, anxiety, and grief through defense mechanisms or coping skills. We stay insanely busy to avoid thinking about or feeling anything unpleasant.

Of course, this doesn't work. What's happening inside just gets stored away to leak out or burst free later.

Yes, I can see that.

I've been there and done that.

I guess that's a form of running from pain.

Yes. Remember that our reflex is to run or to fight.

When it comes to grief, neither of those options works out well for us.

We can learn things like deep breathing. That can be helpful.

We can try to distract ourselves in healthy ways. That can also be helpful.

But coping skills aren't the answer.

So, what is the answer?

23
STUCK IN A CYCLE

I BELIEVE THE ULTIMATE ANSWER TO fear, anxiety, and grief is a solid and dynamic relationship with someone who knows us, loves us, and will always act for our ultimate good.

When we're in a relationship like that, most of our problems solve themselves over time.

Are you saying that we need to be in a close relationship with someone who is perfect, and that perfect someone is God?

Yes, that's what I believe. If we really want to be loved, feel safe, and heal at the heart and soul level, I believe God is the answer.

I can teach you coping skills and any number of techniques for managing fear and anxiety. Again, these things are helpful. But if that's all we have, we're just treating symptoms and not going after the disease. We're just scratching the surface.

I think I get that.

Could you go a little further?

Sure.

Do you ever sense that you're stuck? Stuck in fear? Stuck in anxiety?

Yes. All the time.

Rest assured you're not alone. Most people feel stuck at some point on their grief journey.

However, the reality is that they're circling. They're caught in a cycle of some kind.

Can you give me an example?

24
COPING BUT NOT GOING ANYWHERE

Let's say anxiety is a huge issue in your life.

It is!

Anxiety is a big issue for most of us.

You get anxious. You begin deep breathing. You acknowledge the anxiety. You talk about the anxiety out loud. You try to distract yourself. And so on.

You employ every coping skill you can think of, if you manage to remember any of them in the heat of the battle.

Oh my.

I know exactly what you're saying!

We frantically try to apply all these coping skills to keep the anxiety at bay and attempt to prevent it from totally hijacking us.

Sometimes we're somewhat successful. Other times, it's a total flop.

At best, we might gain a little confidence in handling these crises. But we still get surprised and hijacked. We work hard at coping well, but with limited results.

Many people give up. They don't know what to do, so they settle down into Stuck-Ville and go through the same cycles repeatedly.

I'm not judging anyone. I've cycled around thousands of times. I still struggle with this cope-but-don't-really-go-anywhere cycle.

What a mouthful - the cope-but-don't-really-go-anywhere cycle.

I can relate.

Can you describe that cycle a little more?

25

THERE MUST BE A BETTER WAY

The cope-but-don't-really-go-anywhere cycle basically looks something like this…

Fear, anxiety, or grief get your attention. They exert their influence and sometimes hijack you. You learn a skill to help.

You try hard. You fail. You try harder. You make a tiny bit of progress. You fail. You try another skill. You fail. You try harder. You make a tiny bit of progress. You fail.

"Try harder."

I get it.

I've been through that cycle more times than I can count.

Sadly, that cycle might describe my entire adult life.

You are not alone in that.

Again, I still struggle with my cycles.

So, how do you break that cycle?

You break the cycle by trusting.

Imagine for a moment that you're standing over on the other side of the room.

See yourself going through one of those try-harder-fail cycles. Imagine that cycle goes on and on and on.

What would you say to yourself?

> *What are you doing?*
>
> *Stop it!*
>
> *This isn't working.*
>
> *There must be a better way.*

Exactly.

This isn't working.

There must be a better way.

26
WHAT IF THE ANSWER TO OUR PROBLEM IS A PERSON?

I said before that life is ultimately about relationships. Do you agree with that?

Yes, I think I agree with that.
Life does seem to be about relationships.
We certainly can't survive without them.
We are relational people.

Yes, we are.

We've talked about how the Bible tells us that we're created in the image of God. That means our first and foremost relationship is with the One who created us.

The Bible also says that God is not an impersonal force or power, but a spirit who is also a person. He is perfect, and therefore His love is perfect. Only God knows who we are and why we're here.

Imagine knowing that no matter where you go and what you do, a perfect Person is with you.

This Person knows everything about you, including everything you think and feel.

This Person loves you perfectly and always acts in your ultimate best interest.

This Person knows everything. This Person has perfect and complete knowledge and wisdom.

This Person is available to you 24/7.

This Person created you. This Person has a good plan for your life.

This Person knows the future and loves you perfectly.

This Person wants to guide you so that you can be who you're designed to be and do what you're created to do.

That sounds way too good to be true.

Plus, life is full of pain and junk.

If God is really like that, then why is all this happening?

Great question. For now, can you put that aside? I think you'll be able to answer that question yourself by the end of our conversation.

For now, let's assume that the Bible is God's Word, and that God is telling us the truth.

Can you do that?

27
WHEN FEAR AND ANXIETY STRIKE

Yes, I think I can do that.
I'll certainly try.

God is with you, all the time, everywhere.
When fear strikes, He is with you.
When anxiety hits, He is with you.
When the grief is overwhelming, He's in it with you.
Would knowing that God is with you every moment help you when you're scared or anxious?

I certainly hope so.

If you knew and believed that God loved you perfectly and was with you in a moment of fear, what would you do?

This is hard to imagine.
Is it okay if I think of God as a human - sort of?

Yes, for our purposes, that's okay. In fact, we'll go somewhere with that later.

Breathe deeply for a moment. In through your nose, and out through your mouth.

Good.

Again.

Now, picture a time when you were recently afraid.

Now imagine God, who loves you and knows you completely, was with you in this moment of fear.

What would you do?

28
I WANT TO FEEL SAFE

Okay. I'm imagining God with me in that moment of fear.

I would talk to Him. I would share what's happening inside me.

Since He is the ultimate safe person, I would cry, scream, or whatever.

I would run to Him and want Him to hold me.

I want so badly to feel safe and protected.

Take your time.
Breathe.
Keep breathing.
Stay in that moment, in God's arms.
When you can, tell me what you're feeling.

I want to cry.

There is so much inside me.

I want to let it all out.

Do you think that's because you feel safe right now?

> *I guess so.*

Do you feel loved right now?

> *Yes, I think I do.*

Where do you think that's coming from?

> *I'm so unsure of myself.*
> *God?*
> *Is it coming from God?*

You are seeing yourself in God's arms, right?

> *Yes.*

Take a few moments and rest in His arms. Take as long as you like.

29
I'M SO EMBARRASSED

I'm sorry.

I can't believe I cried like that.

I'm so embarrassed.

I'm proud of you. Getting the grief, fear, anxiety out is an important part of this.

God is not embarrassed. He just wants to comfort you.

You ran into His arms and rested there.

He has been wanting that for you for a very long time.

He loves you.

(Pause)

Now, do you want to hear some more good news?

Of course.

I can always use some good news.

You asked if you could imagine God as a human being.
Well, you just imagined Jesus.

I don't understand.

> *You're going to have to explain that one.*

The Bible says this about Jesus:

"All things were created by Him and for Him, and through Him all things hold together."

What does that sound like to you?

> *It sounds like Jesus created everything, and that everything was created for Him. And that He keeps everything going.*
>
> *Am I right?*
>
> *How is that possible?*

The Bible also says that Jesus, though He was fully God, took on human flesh and became a man.

He was still fully God, but also was fully man.

30
WE HAVE A BIG PROBLEM

So, Jesus is God and human?
I still don't get it.
How is that possible?

Well, if He is God and can do anything, is it possible that He could take on human flesh and remain God?

I guess so.
But why?
Why would God do that?

Because we - you, and I, and every other human being - had a terrible problem that only He could solve.

We had a heart problem. Something was deeply wrong at the core of our being.

Looking at the world today, would you say we have a heart problem?

I never thought about it that way.
What we do and say ultimately comes from inside us.

> *Yes, we clearly have a big problem.*

This heart problem is the source of all our fear, terror, and anxiety. It's also the reason for our unkindness, our abuses, and our two-faced inconsistencies.

In fact, this heart problem is the source of all our personal and relational issues.

> *You said earlier that we need to get past coping mechanisms and go to the real solution.*
>
> *Is that where we're heading?*

Yes. Exactly.

If we're created for relationships, doesn't it make sense that the solution to our problems would be a person - a relationship?

31
WHAT EXACTLY ARE WE CHASING?

Because we're created for relationship, the solution to our problem would need to be a person.

And that person would have to be perfect, which would mean God.

And you're saying that Jesus is God.

Therefore, Jesus is the ultimate answer to my fear and anxiety?

That's what the Bible says, and yes, that's what I believe.

And it's certainly been what I've experienced personally.

It's not about never having any fear, anxiety, or grief. That's not possible in this world.

It's about knowing Jesus and trusting Him.

What does that mean?

How does one do that?

Let's go back to that heart problem we all have.

We all long for certain things. We chase them.

Sometimes we think we've captured it. Then we get disappointed. It just didn't satisfy like we thought it would.

Yes, I see that.

And I've certainly experienced it.

Then we chase something else, with the same result.
Yet few people stop and ask, "What exactly am I chasing?"
What do you think we human beings are ultimately longing for and chasing?

Love.

Perfect love.

I agree.
Now, what if that longing was placed in us?
What if that longing for perfect love is part of being human?
What if we're all really longing for God?

32
LOOKING FOR MEANING AND WORTH

You're saying that God placed a hunger
for perfect love within us.

In other words, He placed a longing in us for Himself.

I follow you.

Keep going.

Now, in your opinion, do people naturally run to God for their meaning and worth?

Are you kidding?

No!

We look in the mirror, at our stuff, and in our bank accounts.

We look for worth in ourselves and in other people.

We look for love anywhere we think we might find it.

What do you think?
How are we doing?

Not very well at all.

I know I'm a mess.

And the world looks worse off than I am.

We don't naturally look to God for love, worth, or meaning.
Instead, we look to almost everyone and everything else.
This is part of our heart problem.
The Bible calls it sin.
When I say the word "sin", what comes to mind?

33
OUR HEART PROBLEM

*Sin is not a nice word. It's considered
a bad word in our society.*

In fact, I don't hear anyone use it anymore.

*When I hear the word "sin", I think of things
like stealing, abuse, and murder.*

Let's take those three actions - stealing, murder, and abuse.

Does a person just wake up one day and steal something, abuse someone, or commit murder?

No, of course not.

Underneath those actions are things like disappointment, hurt, anger, envy, greed, fear, bitterness, and hatred.

These are the things lurking deep in our hearts. In fact, they've been brewing and building there since we were born.

*So, our problem is deeper than our actions.
Our problem is our hearts.*

*If I think about my own pride and what
I've been told, I want to reject that.*

> *If I look at my life and the world out there, however, it's pretty obvious.*
>
> *We've got a deep internal problem that we can't seem to shake.*

Yes, exactly. And if we look at human history, we can see it through all the ages.

Some periods might be better than others, but based on today's world, it's hard to say that mankind has progressed or advanced.

What if our hearts are dead to God?

What if we're expressing that deadness every day?

What if the essence of sin is rejecting God?

> *Ouch. That hurts.*
>
> *But it makes sense.*
>
> *What does rejecting God look like?*

34
TRYING TO DO LIFE WITHOUT GOD

Rejecting God is equivalent to not recognizing or honoring Him for who He is.

The essence of sin is living for ourselves apart from God.

We reject God when we think that this is "our life." We think we can do whatever we want with it.

Then we have all rejected God.

I mean all of us.

Yes, we have.

Our rejection of God expresses the deadness of our hearts. We end up hurting ourselves and other people.

Continual, ongoing rejection of God puts us in a place where we set ourselves up as God.

When that happens, other people and human life have less and less value.

What do you think about that?

It's disturbing.

I can see it in the world.

Sadly, I can see it in myself.

I've tried to do life without God, well, all the time.

And yet, I've had a pretty good life in many ways.

Yes. The truly good things in life all come from God. He blesses all of us.

He loves us. He gives us life. He has given us every good ability we have. He enables us to live, work, and relate to others.

Even though people don't know Him or choose to reject Him, He is still there, blessing them every day.

But they are missing out. They are missing out on a relationship with God and all that comes with that.

Without God, their longings will never be fulfilled. They will never know true peace apart from Him.

Their hearts will remain dead. And they will continue to live out that deadness in their lives and relationships.

My mind keeps coming up with questions.

It keeps saying, "No, this can't be right."

But something deep inside me resonates with all of this.

35
THE ULTIMATE SOLUTION

I think what I'm saying resonates with you because it comes from God's Word, the Bible. I'm simply stating what God has revealed in His Word.

When people continue to reject God, eventually things get much worse.

As they reject His goodness and His mercy, they begin to experience more of the results of rejecting Him.

Their deadness becomes even more apparent. I believe that's what we're seeing in our world today.

> *Things are bad, and they seem to be getting worse.*
>
> *If our hearts are the problem, what's the solution?*
>
> *You've said the solution to fear and anxiety*
> *- and everything else - is God.*
>
> *You've also said that Jesus is God, and*
> *therefore Jesus is the solution.*
>
> *Have I understood you correctly?*

Yes. Again, this is not my opinion. This is written all over the pages of the Bible.

How is Jesus the solution?

If Jesus is God in human flesh, then it is possible for Him to live a perfect, sinless life. After all, He is perfect. He is fully human as well as fully God.

Okay.

If He is God, and God is perfect and can do anything, then that would be logically possible.

The Bible says that Jesus died for us on the cross. You've probably heard that phrase from someone at some point.

What that means is that He took all our sin and all our deadness on Himself and died in our place.

The Bible says that He willingly laid down His life for us out of love - perfect love.

He did that for me. He did that for you.

What's happening inside you right now?

36
WHAT IF?

*It feels like a battle is going on in my
heart. A huge tug-of-war.*

*It's like I'm leaning forward into all this, but at
the same time something is holding me back.*

Breathe for a moment.

That's good.

Again. Breathe slowly and deeply.

Okay. I'm ready.

Please go on.

What if Jesus is God - the One who thought of you, planned you, and created you?

What if Jesus came here, lived a perfect life, and then died on the cross to solve your sin and your deadness?

What if, because He is God, death had no hold on Him? What if He rose from the dead and conquered death?

What if Jesus did all of this for you, and there's nothing you need to do but receive it for what it is - a gift?

What if the real gift is Himself?

What if the things that every person desperately needs and longs for - forgiveness, perfect love, and eternal life - are all in Jesus?

What if He is right here in this room right now?

What would you say to Him?

Yes.

I would say, "Yes."

Did you say that to me, or to Him?

To Him.

37
PEACEFUL, ACCEPTED, AND FREE

I don't know how to describe this.
I feel different. Very different.
I feel peaceful, and I know this peace did not come from me.
I feel accepted, welcomed, and loved.
I feel free.

Do you believe Jesus came for you, died for you, and rose from the dead for you?

Do you sense you have responded to His invitation to come to Him?

Yes.

Yes, I do.

I saw Him standing in front of me with open arms.

I just walked into His embrace.

I feel safe.

Jesus drew you to Himself. You responded.

You are now in His embrace. He is freedom, safety, and peace.

He is salvation from sin. He is eternal life.

He is your Savior. He is your Lord. He created you. He knows you.

And now, you know Him.

Yes, I do.

Not very well, but I know Him.

You will get to know Him better, much better.

It's like any other relationship. The more time you spend with Him, the better you will know Him.

For now, just close your eyes and enjoy Him.

Rest in Him.

Receive His goodness, mercy, and favor.

Rest in His perfect love.

38
A CHANGE IN IDENTITY

Somehow, things have changed.

I mean, things haven't changed out there. The world is the same. My circumstances are the same.

But things have changed in here, inside me.

When we respond to Jesus' invitation to trust Him, He gives us a new heart.

You are now new. Your spirit, the deepest part of you, your spirit is new.

Your identity has changed.

Tell me more about that.

I feel like the same me, but different at the same time.

You belong to God now. You are His child. He is your Father. And He is a perfect Father.

Jesus is not only with you, but now He is also in you. And you are in Him.

In fact, the Bible says that you are now one spirit with Him. You are united with Him on the deepest possible level.

It all sounds too good, but I know it is true.

I just know it.

Yes. The Bible says that everything has changed for you now. You are fundamentally different. You are new.

Jesus said that when someone trusts Him, they receive His life – eternal life. They have crossed over from death to life.

You are in Jesus now, and nothing can separate you from Him or His love.

It's not about you and what you've done or haven't done. It's about Him and what He has done for you.

Life is about Jesus. He is life.

39
A CONTINUAL CONVERSATION

So, what do I do now?

You get to know Jesus better.

You learn to rest in Him and to trust Him.

You talk to Him in much the same way you're talking to me. That's called prayer.

You listen to Him. He is always speaking to you through what He has already spoken.

That's the Bible.

Let life become a continual conversation with Him. You're learning to do life with Jesus now.

Or, I should say, Jesus is teaching you to do life with Him.

That makes sense.

*The Bible is a big book. I've tried to
read some of it in the past.*

It was frustrating. I didn't understand it.

That's common for a lot of people.

Now that Jesus lives in you, He will be teaching you as you read.

Keep in mind that the Bible is really all about Him. He reveals Himself and His plan for us through its pages.

When you read it, try to picture Jesus speaking directly to you.

Do you think you can do that?

I can sure try.

That certainly sounds better than plodding through a huge, intimidating book.

Take it a little at a time.

Where you start is important too. I would recommend you begin with the Gospel of Luke in the New Testament.

Luke is one of the accounts of Jesus' life here on earth. As you read, try to focus on receiving rather than understanding everything.

When I read, I try to focus on listening to Jesus' voice. Reading His Word is spending focused time with Him.

When I read, I'm listening to my Creator, Savior, and best friend.

That sounds so good.

I'll try that.

40
A COMPLETELY SECURE FUTURE

Now, let's focus again on what's real.

Jesus is in this room with us.

He is also in me. And now, He is in you.

I am also in Him. You are in Him, too.

You are loved, saved, and safe.

You have a completely secure future with Him.

I think it's going to take a while for all this to sink in.

Yet, I feel it. I sense it.

I know it's true.

That's Jesus in you - the Holy Spirit - speaking to you, comforting you, and strengthening you.

Life is now about Him and allowing Him to work in and through you.

Let me get this straight. Jesus is the ultimate answer to dealing with fear, anxiety, and grief.

When I read the Bible, I'm really listening to Jesus' voice.

> *When I talk to Him, I'm praying.*
>
> *And it's okay that I don't understand everything. After all, how could I?*

Exactly.

Another important way to know Jesus better is being with other people who know Him, love Him, and are following Him.

Now, a lot of people call themselves Christians, but they may not know Jesus. They might know a lot about Jesus, but that doesn't mean they have a personal relationship with Him.

41
RELIGION VERSES RELATIONSHIP

I think I've met some of those people. They call themselves Christians, but they don't act like it.

Are they Christians in name only? Is it that they're just not serious about their faith?

They might be serious about church or about religion, but that still doesn't mean they know Jesus or have a relationship with Him.

They might be trying hard. Some are attempting to earn their way into heaven.

For others, churchgoing and religion are merely for show - a mask they wear from time to time.

I know a lot of people who want nothing to do with Jesus because they see so much hypocrisy in Christians.

My personal experience is that religious people can be some of the most judgmental and unkind people around.

Sadly, that's my experience too.

We get into trouble when we confuse religion with relationship.

Religion is about rules. Religion is about doing this and not doing that. Religion is about rituals.

Religion is about earning points so that hopefully, when the time comes, we'll have done enough.

But that's the exact opposite of what we've been talking about.

The Bible says we can't earn our way. We're spiritually dead.

We can't do anything. God must do it all.

Yes, exactly. And God did it all, through Jesus Christ.

On the cross, just before He died, Jesus said, "It is finished."

It is done. God did it.

42
THE TREADMILL OF PERFORMANCE

A RELATIONSHIP WITH JESUS CHRIST BEGINS with the word, "Done."

Religion, on the other hand, is all about the word, "Do."

A relationship with Jesus is about what He did for us and wants to do in and through us.

Religion is about what we must do and should do to be better humans.

> *That's a big difference.*
>
> *Those systems conflict with each other, don't they?*

Yes, they do.

One system is about God pursuing people and people responding to Him.

The other is about people trying to get to God or to be God through their own efforts.

> *And if I start focusing on what I should be doing, doesn't that take the focus off Jesus and what He did for me?*

> *I would think that, after a while, everything becomes about performance. And then we're right back in that cycle of try, fail, try harder, fail.*

Yes. And with that cycle comes an onslaught of fear, anxiety, and anger.

Imagine being an orphan. A loving father adopts you. He welcomes you into his home, provides for you, protects you, and loves you wholeheartedly.

Now, imagine you wake up one morning and the first thing you see is a list of rules. This list is titled, "Things You Have to Do to Keep Me as Your Father and to Stay in My Family."

What would you think about that? How would you feel?

> *I would be terrified.*
>
> *I would begin living in fear of losing this wonderful father and new family.*
>
> *I would start working hard right away.*
>
> *I would be anxious all the time, wondering if I was doing enough.*
>
> *And finally, I would be angry and depressed. I would never feel good enough.*

That's exactly what happens to a lot of religious people.

43
WALKING THROUGH THE FIRE

It's so easy to get caught in that religious performance cycle.

It's so easy to make it about us and what we do rather than about Jesus and what He has done and wants to do.

Freedom comes when we take our eyes off ourselves and the world around us and gaze at Jesus. Only then can things begin to make sense.

> *I understand what you're saying. I need to be around people who love Jesus and are following Him.*
>
> *How do I find people like that? In churches? If so, what kind of church?*

There are some great, Jesus-following Bible teachers out there. I can give you one or two to check out.

And yes, you can find loving Jesus-followers in many churches.

The thing to keep in mind is that churches are full of people. People, even those who follow Jesus closely, are not Jesus.

People are imperfect, even the wonderful ones. People will disappoint us. Churches and church leaders will disappoint us.

Jesus, however, will never disappoint you. Life, situations, and circumstances will disappoint you, but Jesus never will.

Now, how can I say that?

Well, if Jesus is God and He loves me perfectly, then He will always do the most loving thing for me, right?

Right.

Then if I'm personally disappointed, it just means that I don't fully get what Jesus is doing and how He will use that for my good.

Am I on the right track?

Definitely.

We trust Jesus with our circumstances. His love and care are not circumstantial or situational.

He does not always save us from the fire but walks with us through the fire.

Hardship is an opportunity to trust Jesus, to know Him better, and to begin to live above and beyond our circumstances.

44
LIGHT IN THE DARKNESS

Think about it this way.

Imagine yourself in the middle of thick, overgrown forest. It's dark and a bit foreboding. There's a barely visible path in front of you. You've never been here before.

Can you see that?

Yes. Easily.

Now, see Jesus with you there.

In the Bible, Jesus says, "I am the light of the world. Whoever follows me will never walk in darkness but have the light of life."

Jesus is the light of the world. He is light. He is your light.

Now, what do you see?

I'm in the dark forest.

*Trees are crowding in all around me.
There is overgrowth everywhere.*

When I saw Jesus, a light began to shine.

The light got brighter and brighter. It got so bright that I couldn't see the forest anymore.

> *I could only see Jesus.*

Good.

Now, as we've said before, the Bible says that you are in Jesus, and that He is in you.

Picture yourself in Him somehow.

> *I see myself surrounded by Him.*
> *I'm completely immersed in light.*

And what about the forest?

> *I can see the forest, but I'm looking at it through His light.*
> *And the forest looks different.*
> *It's the same forest, but it's not dark and scary anymore.*

Now picture Jesus in you.
What do you see?

> *Light shooting out of me in all directions, lighting up the forest.*
> *This light is coming from Jesus in me.*
> *I see the path more clearly now.*
> *The forest is no longer frightening. It doesn't matter that I have never been here before.*
> *Jesus is with me and in me.*

45
NOT A WAY OUT BUT A WAY THROUGH

Now, tell me what you think the point of all that was.

Is the forest my life and the world?

Or maybe the forest is this whole grief process?

Things certainly look dark and foreboding. I'm not sure which way to take. It's lonely. And I can't see the path ahead.

But Jesus knows this forest. He knows everything.

It's not about finding a way out of the forest, but rather walking with Jesus through the forest.

Did I get it?

I wasn't looking for one specific answer, but you certainly got the idea.

And Jesus spoke to you through the process and gave you some wisdom.

We know the world is a mess and getting messier. Things appear dark and seem to be getting darker.

We also know that the grief process is challenging, painful, and messy. Each loss is uncharted territory for our hearts.

Jesus is the light of the world. He is your constant companion and guide. He lives in you, and you live in Him.

He can handle whatever fear, anxiety, and grief this forest might bring.

> *I like the picture of the dark forest. It's a lot like life.*
>
> *The path is barely visible and continually winding.*
>
> *You only see the steps ahead by taking the step right in front of you.*
>
> *You can plan all you want in this world, but everything can change in an instant.*
>
> *And since Jesus is in me and I'm in Him, I always have plenty of light.*

I like that picture too. And I like how you're thinking about it.

Even in a dark forest, with Jesus there's plenty of light. No matter what trouble the forest holds, Jesus is fully aware of it.

He will guide you through and use every bit of trouble for His own good purposes in your life.

Are you ready for another picture?

> *Sure.*

46
FEAR AND DIVISION

Imagine a city street.

Picture a street in a major city. People are everywhere.

It's dark on this city street, but it's not night. People are walking here and there like this darkness in the daytime is normal.

Things slowly became darker over time, and they grew accustomed to the darkness.

People are moving and bumping into each other here and there, but no one is interacting. No one is really looking at anyone else.

Many of them are on their phones as they walk. Interestingly, their phones do not emit light, but rather only more darkness.

Are you with me so far?

Oh yes.

This feels very close to reality.

See yourself in the middle of the street watching all this.
See Jesus with you.
Remember, He is the light.
See yourself not just with Jesus, but in Him. See Him in you.
Now, look at the street through Him and His light.

What do you see?

> *I see behind people's facial expressions.*
>
> *I see great sadness and confusion. Terrible fear and anxiety. Anger and rage.*
>
> *It feels like many are on the edge - like they're about to lose control somehow.*
>
> *It feels as if the whole street is about to explode.*
>
> *I see them turning on each other and fights breaking out. Everyone is shouting and yelling.*
>
> *Some people fight in groups, but no one helps anyone else.*
>
> *It's like they're all alone. Every one of them.*

I can see that as you describe it.

When we walk with Jesus and allow Him to show us things through His light, we see life with much greater clarity.

Do you feel like what you're seeing is happening in our world?

> *Oh yes. And much more. Much worse.*
>
> *Don't get me wrong. There's a lot of good out there - I guess. But everyone seems stressed, fearful, and angry.*
>
> *I know many are teetering on the edge of hopelessness and despair.*
>
> *Everyone is so divided.*

47
WALKING IN THE LIGHT

Now, let's go back to that picture of the city street.

See yourself in Jesus, and Him in you. You are looking through His light.

Start walking down the street. Ask Jesus to lead you. Follow Him.

He leads you up to a person who is angry and raving. Their face is distorted by their rage. They scream that you're the problem - that you're the reason they're angry.

Wow. I don't have any fear because I'm in Jesus.

I know their anger is not about me. It's about them.

Good. They get frustrated because they can't fluster you or get to you. Finally, they walk away.

You have, I'm sure, encountered people who don't understand or accept your grief. Some even get angry with you for grieving.

When they see you, they feel things they don't want to feel - their own sadness, grief, and longings. Their reactions are about them, not about you.

Back on the city street, Jesus leads you to another person.

This person is terrified. They're so scared that they can't even look at you. They turn and walk away, looking all around and behind them as they go.

So sad. I've been there.

I could feel some of their fear and anxiety.

I wish they hadn't walked away.

I know. The answer to their fear and terror was right in front of them.

Some people are blinded by fear. Jesus' arms are open. Many simply walk on by.

Jesus leads you to another person. This person is disturbed and sad. They are troubled by what's happening around them. They see you and make eye contact.

They look into your eyes for a moment. They feel drawn to you. You have a conversation. Jesus touches them through you.

I never thought about anything like that before.

I never considered that Jesus could touch others through me.

I mean, of course He can, because He can do anything.
I guess it just hadn't dawned on me before.

Yes, Jesus can use you in the lives of others - more than you can imagine.

Jesus leads you further down the street, and the person you are conversing with decides to walk with you.

You look ahead and see someone who is shining. This shining one knows Jesus. He is shining in and through them.

This shining person comes up to you and your companion and greets you both with a smile. It feels as if you they know you, and that you know them. They know Jesus, who is in you.

You talk and walk together for a bit. The other person with you continues to tag along, drawn by the light in both of you.

As the three of you walk along, the light coming from the two of you who know Jesus gets brighter.

The crowd on the street sees this.

Some people stop and stare.

Others glance your direction, then return their gaze to their dark phones and keep walking.

Some turn away from you and go the opposite direction.

Now, focus on being in Jesus and Him being in you. Rest in His love and peace.

Breathe.

48
A NEW LIFE AND A NEW HOME

I think I get it.

The world is a dark place. Jesus is the light of the world.

He lives in me. He shines in and through me, even while I'm grieving.

The people around me will respond in different ways to Jesus' light. Some will be drawn to the light. Others will be repelled by it.

People's reactions to me are not about me, but about them - who they are and where they are spiritually.

My job is to rest in Jesus and walk with Him.

Beautifully said.

Whatever may come, Jesus is with you and in you. You are in Him. Life is about a relationship with Him.

He is life. He is your life. He is your home.

Jesus is my home.

That's a new thought.

I like that.

I want to think about that more.

Think about it this way. God thought of you before He created the universe. He wanted you and planned you. He knew you.

At just the right time, He created you in your mother's womb. Ultimately, you are not from here. You are from God.

In other words, this place is not your home. It never has been.

But of course, you thought it was your home, so you tried to make it your home.

How did that work out?

Lousy.

I pushed and strove.

I worked and achieved.

I chased relentlessly after things that promised happiness and meaning, but I was never satisfied.

In the end, it was all empty.

And now, it seems like it's all disappearing.

When we think of this place as our home, our hearts become rooted in this world. We become enslaved to houses, possessions, comfort, jobs, entertainment, etc.

We can lose all these things. They are temporary. They can be taken from us.

I also immersed myself in a few people to the point that I probably made them my life - my purpose.

These people either disappointed me, left, or died. When they left, so did my meaning and purpose.

It's easy for us to elevate the people we love above God.

We cling to the immediate blessing right in front of us and miss the One who blessed us with that relationship in the first place.

When the blessing disappears, we're left devastated and even hopeless.

You just described me.

I've been there, and I can be there again in a heartbeat.

49

ON ASSIGNMENT AWAY FROM HOME

Again, we are not from this place. This place is not our home. We are passing through.

As believers in Jesus, we are currently on assignment away from home.

We're on a mission in a foreign land.

I like that.

I am on assignment away from home.

That makes sense.

If this world is not my home, that changes everything. If this is temporary lodging, I should be traveling as light as possible.

As it is, I've burdened myself with stuff that doesn't matter. I've also allowed myself to be burdened by others and the world.

I feel like I've wasted so much of my life.

I can relate to what you're saying. We all could have done better.

In Jesus, we are forgiven and free from the past. He can use our past for His purposes.

As He guides you, He will enable you to let the past go and focus on Him in the present.

Don't spend too much time looking in the rear-view mirror. Just glance there when you need to. Gaze through the windshield and keep your eyes on Jesus.

Jesus will continue to remind you of who you are now. Listen to Him. Take it in. Let it sink down into the deepest part of you.

You are His. You are a child of God. You are forgiven.

You are in Jesus, and He is in you. You now have His life - eternal life.

You are a foreigner and stranger here. Have you ever felt like you didn't belong?

Yes. All the time.

As I think about what I did just to try and belong, I shudder.

I felt left out often in my life. I felt different and on the outside of things.

I was successful and extremely busy, but never content or satisfied.

That's why my loss hurts so much. With that person, I felt like I belonged.

When we lose someone like that, it's almost like a part of us dies too.

Since each person is unique, they have their own place in our hearts. These people are gifts from God to us.

When we try to make our home here, as if this is all there is, we're never content or satisfied. We might feel good for a little while, but it doesn't last.

We all hunger to belong. We all feel left out. It never dawns on us that the problem is in our own hearts.

A few other people might love us and help us feel like we belong. But then something happens. They leave or die. We can feel deeply alone.

When we come to know Jesus, our perspective changes. We begin to look more through eternal lenses rather than the lenses of time. We begin to make decisions like people who have a forever future somewhere else. We begin to release things here and invest in things there.

Imagine all the fear, anxiety, and grief that comes from trying to figure things out and make this place our permanent home.

We're beating our heads against the wall, and we're clueless about it.

50
AN ETERNAL MINDSET

*Things only seem to make sense for me when
I realize this world is not my home.*

So much perspective comes from that.

I have trouble hanging onto that though.

I blink, and that eternal mindset disappears.

Join the club. We all struggle with that.

Thankfully, it's not about getting it right or perfect. It's just about walking with Jesus.

As we get to know Him, we become more like Him.

We experience more and more of Him.

We learn to trust Him more and more.

It's not about you or your performance. It's about Jesus and His love for you.

I get so easily distracted.

If I look at the world at all, my heart gets rattled.

*I don't want to be rattled, but I can't help but feel a little
of the fear, anger, and anxiety that are out there.*

Things feel uncertain, unsafe, and unpredictable.

I can understand that. It doesn't take me long to get upset either. There's so much pain, division, and terror out there.

You're right. We live in this world, even though this is not our home.

Are you ready for another picture?

Sure.

In the New Testament book of Hebrews, God tells us this: "Therefore, since we are surrounded by such a great cloud of witnesses, let us throw off everything that hinders and the sin that so easily entangles. And let us run with perseverance the race marked out for us…"

The picture here is of an ancient stadium. The stadium packed with spectators. A race is being run.

You are there. You are running this race.

Can you picture that?

Yes, but I'm not much of a runner.

Me either. Ugh. But let's go with it.

51
RUNNING THE RACE

As you run this race, you are surrounded by a great crowd of witnesses. These are believers in Jesus through the ages that are now with Him in heaven.

These followers were faithful. They endured incredible hardships. Many of them were even killed for their faith.

These are our brothers and sisters in faith who have gone before us.

This might be stretching it a bit, but the context seems to suggest that these folks are cheering you on.

Wow.

Okay. I can see that.

Now, see yourself trying to run this race with ropes loosely wrapped around your legs.

A couple of heavy ankle weights are strapped onto your ankles too.

Also, a heavy, overflowing cart is attached to your torso.

Oh, and you're blindfolded.

(Pause)

How are you doing?

Not very well at all.

I'm exhausting myself while barely moving.

It's a funny picture, but a sad one.

Now, you take off the blindfold.

You get your bearings and then look down the track in front of you. Jesus is there, waving you on.

Of course, Jesus is everywhere, so He's right there beside you too. And He's in you as well.

You begin trying to run to Jesus. You stumble forward, struggling against all that's wrapped around you.

You call out to Jesus. He smiles.

The ropes, ankle weights, and cart harness fall from you. You're free.

You begin walking toward Jesus.

At first, it's tough. You haven't been able to walk well with all those weights and hindrances. The more you walk, the easier it gets.

Finally, you begin to jog and then run.

Can you see it?

Yes.

I feel like I'm getting a workout.

52
DODGING DISTRACTIONS

Suddenly, people start running onto the track from every direction.

They're shouting at you and trying to get your attention.

These are not the people in the stands cheering you on. These people are trying to get you to stop running.

Obstacles appear on the track too. Lots of them. These are the things of this world - money, possessions, achievement, comfortability, etc.

The track is now crowded and extremely noisy.

You look down the track, and there's Jesus. You fix your eyes on Him.

See yourself ignoring all the noise and distractions. You begin to resolutely run toward Jesus.

As you run, a few things along the way manage to distract you and pull your eyes away from Jesus.

You stumble and sometimes fall.

You get up, fix your eyes on Jesus again, and continue running toward Him.

I can see that. I get it, I think.

The world is full of noise and distraction. All that matters is Jesus and keeping my eyes on Him.

As I do that, life will make more sense. My purpose will be clearer. My sense of meaning will be richer.

And I will experience more of Jesus and His peace.

Yes. Exactly.

In those verses in Hebrews, it also said that you are running "the race marked out for you."

What does that phrase tell you?

That God knows everything.

He is not surprised by the hindrances, obstacles, and distractions on the track.

The race has been marked out for me.

Jesus is both my companion and my goal.

Yes. Jesus is with you, in you, and ahead of you and waiting for you.

You run with Him, for Him, and to Him.

53
FACING OPPOSITION

In those verses in Hebrews, we're also told, "Consider Jesus, who endured such opposition from sinners, so that you will not grow weary and lose heart."

We live in tough, challenging times. Given mankind's spiritual deadness and sin problem, things will probably get worse.

You will face opposition for your beliefs. Following Jesus will not be popular.

People may pull away from you. Some may even view you as a threat of some kind, even when all you want to do is love them.

Other people will come to you, especially those who see your hope and are drawn to the light in you.

Keep your eyes on Jesus and run the race before you.

Yes, I'm already experiencing these things.

People are angry. People judge, label, and categorize each other.

Many people's minds seem closed. Their hearts seem closed too, even hard.

No one seems interested in understanding anything,

*but everybody is eager to share their opinion.
And yet, most opinions seem to be parroted
from whatever media they're exposed to.*

*It's getting to the point where a person can't ask a question
or voice a concern. All attempts at dialog get shut down.*

Whatever happened to agreeing to disagree?

It feels like we're losing our humanity.

Yes, I see that too.

The Bible tells that it will be this way. As you said, God is not surprised.

Jesus is still at work. He is the light of the world.

Our job is to rest in Him, live in Him, know Him, and walk with Him.

As we do that, He will shine in and through us.

Our future, your future, is secure in Him.

54
RELENTLESS LOVE

I'm reading my Bible every day, a little bit at a time. I don't understand everything, but I do sense Jesus speaking to me.

I keep reminding myself that it's not my responsibility to get it or to figure it out.

It's my job to listen, trust, and follow.

Yes, it's all about Jesus. Again, He is the answer, the antidote, the remedy.

You have Jesus. Therefore, you have everything.

I am discovering that all things that are worth having are in Him - love, peace, joy, endurance, kindness, compassion, goodness, gentleness, patience, and everything good.

Yes, indeed.

Jesus came and gave His life for you, so that He could give His life to you, so that He could live His life in and through you.

He thought of you, planned you, and created you. He came to earth and went to the cross thinking about you. He conquered death for you.

He is preparing a place for you. He will come back to get you, so that you may be with Him forever.

Some days, I want to pinch myself. Is this really true?

God pursued me. Jesus initiated a relationship with me. Jesus knocked on my heart's door. And He just kept knocking.

His love is beautifully relentless.

I'm so glad I know Him.

He is mine, and I am His.

And that is all that matters.

55
FOCUSING ON THE GOAL

*You said that Jesus will come back and
take me to be with Him.*

Could you tell me more about that?

I'll let Jesus tell you about that.

Here's what He says in John chapter 14:

"Do not let your hearts be troubled. Believe in God, believe also in Me. In my Father's house are many rooms. If this were not so, I would have told you. I go now to prepare a place for you. And if I go to prepare a place for you, I will come back to take you, so that you also may be where I am."

He is preparing a place for you. And He's coming back to get you.

"I will come back to take you, so that you also may be where I am."

The goal from the beginning has been that you would know Him and be with Him forever.

This is what you were made for.

So, Jesus thought of me, wanted me, planned me, and

created me. He did all that so that I would have the opportunity to discover Him, know Him, and follow Him.

> *He lives in me. He wants to live through me. He knows me completely. He loves me and is preparing a place for me, with Him.*

> *Currently, I am away from home on assignment. But one day, Jesus will come and pick me up. And I will be with Him forever.*

> *Is that what we're saying? Have I got that right?*

That's what God says in His Word. That's what Jesus says.

In the meantime, you rest in Him, trust Him, and ask Him to work through you.

> *And as I get to know Jesus, the other things will fall into place?*

> *The better I know Him, the more I will trust Him. And the more I trust Him, the more I will experience Him and His love, joy, and peace.*

> *Right?*

Absolutely. It's all about a relationship with Him.

It's not about getting better. It's not about protecting yourself. It's not about never being sad, afraid, anxious, depressed, or angry again.

It's about walking with Jesus, trusting Him, and following Him.

> *It's about running the race marked out for me and keeping my eyes on the goal: Jesus.*

Yes. That's it.

56
TROUBLE WILL COME

You said that it's not about eliminating sadness, fear, anxiety, or anger. It's about focusing on Jesus.

He is the answer to these things, but just because I know Him doesn't mean I will never be sad, fearful, anxious, or angry again.

Is that what we're saying?

Yes. Believing in Jesus is not a magic pill that eliminates all our struggles.

In fact, it is our struggles, our weaknesses, that keep us yearning to connect with Him.

Anxiety, fear, anger, guilt, shame, sadness, depression, and grief can be the fuel that propels us to Jesus and His love.

So, grief, sadness, anxiety, and fear will come.

Yes, they will. The world is still the world, and you are still living here.

But you have options now that you didn't have before. And those options make a huge difference.

Now, Jesus walks with you in that anxiety, fear, and grief.

You can talk to Him about what's happening inside you.

You can release things to Him. You can begin to let go of painful pieces of the past.

Whenever anxiety, fear, or grief knocks, the Creator of the universe is right here with you.

> *So, Jesus doesn't necessarily deliver me from these things, but walks with me in them.*
>
> *And as I choose to trust Him, these things will, over time, have less power over me.*

You've got it. Exactly.

Just because you know Jesus doesn't mean you're any less dependent on Him. In fact, you'll see more and more just how dependent on Him you really are.

Being dependent on Jesus is not weakness. He is God. You are His creation.

Acknowledging that is lining yourself up with truth and true strength.

Your strength comes from Him. He is your strength.

57
MEETING CHALLENGES HEAD ON

It seems that God's goal for me is not to learn to deal with the issues of life - like fear, anxiety, and grief - but rather to get to know Him and walk with Him.

As I do that, He works in me to produce the results He wants in my life.

Yes.

Again, life only makes sense when we let it be about Jesus.

If we don't, we will make life all about us. That's when things get confusing.

Making life about ourselves only fuels the fires of anxiety, fear, sadness, guilt, shame, and depression.

Yes, I can see that.

So, life is not about avoiding trouble, pain, and grief.

It sounds silly when I hear it come out of my mouth.

I've been trying to avoid trouble, loss, and pain all my life.

It's so different to think of trouble, loss, and pain

*as inevitable. I can meet them head on with Jesus
and trust Him with whatever is happening.*

In the book of James in the New Testament, it says this:

"Consider it pure joy, brothers and sisters, when you encounter various trials of many kinds."

Not exactly our typical response to difficulty and hardship, right?

James goes on:

"For you know that the testing of your faith produces perseverance. Let perseverance finish its work, that you may be mature and complete, not lacking in anything."

What do you get from that?

*It sounds like difficulty and hardship are part
of God's training program to mature me.*

*If I let it, hardship can move me to run to
Jesus, seek Him, and trust Him more.*

Exactly.

You're in God's training program. Jesus knows that the absolute best thing for you is to get to know Him better and trust Him more. That pays off not only in this life, but in eternity.

In fact, it pays better than any other investment you could possibly make.

58
PROBLEMS ARE OPPORTUNITIES

You're saying that difficulties - like anxiety, fear, grief, guilt, relational problems, and financial issues - are all opportunities to walk with Jesus and know Him better.

Yes. As you walk with Jesus in and through these things, He develops perseverance in you.

You begin to see things more clearly. Your perspective becomes more eternal. You begin to understand more of God's heart.

He works in you and lives through you more and more.

I think I get it.

I'm on a steep learning curve.

I'm glad Jesus is in charge and that He loves me.

Even though there's a lot of evil out there and terrible things happen every day?

Ahh, yes. I did have that question, didn't I - about how God could be good when things seem so bad?

Well, now I get it, at least somewhat.

We're created in the image of God and part of that means we have a will. We make decisions.

We rejected God along the way. We decided to go it on our own and do life apart from Him.

We elevate ourselves, our ideas, our goals, our desires, other people, possessions, and even nature above God Himself. We consistently choose to worship created things rather than the Creator.

We're broken, and we express our brokenness all the time in all kinds of ways.

God honors the choices we make.

If we choose to walk away from Him and go it on our own, we will experience the results of that. We will express our separation from Him in our thoughts, words, and actions in our families, relationships, and careers.

We choose our own limited wisdom and abilities over Him. If we're separated from Him and His life, the results in our lives and in the world will reflect that.

No wonder we're in such a mess.

We're reaping the results of our own choices.

I'm sure I'll have more questions about all this, but right now my heart is grateful and overflowing.

I'm content to know that there will be an ultimate end to all evil and that God Himself will bring that about.

I want to let Him teach me, rather than me trying to figure it all out.

I can relate. I often try to figure things out on my own. No wonder I wind up scratching my head, confused, and upset.

God knows. He knows it all. As I seek Him first and trust Him, life begins to fall into place.

59
PAIN FEELS DIFFERENT WHEN WALKING IN THE LIGHT

Keep listening to Jesus by immersing yourself in His Word.

Talk to Him about anything and everything.

Keep connecting with other Jesus-followers.

He is with you. His love for you is perfect.

Nothing can separate you from His love.

And some day, perhaps very soon, He is going to come back and pick you up.

(Pause)

Life is challenging. The world is shaking.

As you look at the world out there now, what do you think?

Trouble is everywhere.

I sense anger and hatred more than anything else.

Underneath the rage, I sense fear and terror. Insecurity and terrible pain.

> *The world looks dark - and it's getting darker every day.*
>
> *I'm to be aware of the world, but not focused on it. I am to fix my eyes on Jesus. I am to run the race with Him, toward Him.*
>
> *He is getting closer every day, every hour.*

How does all this influence how you see your loss?

> *It still hurts badly, but pain feels different when you're walking in the light.*
>
> *Jesus is my life now. My life is not in any other single person, as wonderful and loving as they might be.*
>
> *My loved one was an indescribable blessing in my life. My loved one was thought of, planned, and created by God Himself. I'm so grateful.*
>
> *As I get to know Jesus and He develops in me an eternal mindset, this awful loss is beginning to take its proper place in my life.*
>
> *Am I making sense?*

Yes, you are.

It's only when we look at life and other people more through the lens of eternity that we begin to see things even remotely accurately.

The grief road is long. In this life, you will always grieve on some level because you will always miss the people you lose.

Because of Jesus, you won't be missing them for long.

60
FEELING OUT OF PLACE

The more time goes on, the more I feel out of place here.
And the more I feel out of place here, the more meaning my life here has.

Yes, because Jesus lives in you, He is always at work in and through you.

It's dark out there, and He is shining through you.

Now matters.

Everything counts.

I'm starting to see that.
How I think matters.
How I speak matters.
What I do and how I treat others matters.
I want it all to count. Everything.

We have great hope.

The word "hope" in our Bibles actually means "certainty." It means something completely different than our English word "hope."

For example, I might hope it will rain today. By that, I mean I would prefer it to rain, but it might not. In English, hope is wishful thinking.

In the New Testament, however, "hope" refers to something that is sure and certain but hasn't happened yet.

Biblical hope is eternal reality waiting to play out in space and time.

> *So, when we hope for Jesus' return, we're saying that we're looking forward to it as a sure and certain event.*
>
> *And we can have this kind of hope because God is certain. Jesus is certain.*

Yes.

Our faith is built on certainties. We believe God has revealed all this in the Bible.

Of course, we accept this by faith. As we get to know Jesus, we become more convinced of the truth of all these things.

> *But our faith wavers. Some days, I feel like I'm stumbling more than walking.*
>
> *Do you have any doubts?*
>
> *Do you still have questions about all this?*

I wonder about a lot of things. And yes, I have a lot of questions.

I struggle with all kinds of stuff daily.

Yet somehow, as I walk with Jesus, the questions and wonderings seem to matter less and less over time.

I'll be glad to share my questions and wonderings sometime, if you think it would be helpful to you.

Most of my struggles are of my own creation.

I certainly get that.

I'm an expert at problem creation.

We humans are good at that, aren't we?

I'm glad our hope is not in this world. Can you imagine if it was?

In some senses, this world has nothing for us.

We are strangers here. We are away from home on assignment.

We're looking forward to seeing Jesus, face-to-face.

At the end of the last book of the Bible, Revelation, Jesus says, "Yes, I am coming soon."

And the response is, "Amen - so be it. Come, Lord Jesus."

So be it. Come, Lord Jesus.

GARY'S STORY

Thank you for reading this book. I hope you found these pages healing, encouraging, and comforting. If you haven't already, I hope you will embrace Jesus soon.

In fact, I'm praying for you right now.

A CHILDHOOD OF LOSS

My story began with an early childhood of mixed messages and sexual abuse. There were multiple perpetrators and the abuse continued for several years. All the perpetrators were family members. This skewed everything - how I viewed family, people, life, and God. Throughout my childhood I felt dirty, damaged, and different.

I lost both grandfathers so early I barely remember them. Due to dementia, one grandmother never knew who I was. My parents' marriage was strained and volatile. I never knew what to expect.

Looking back, I can see that my mom had been slipping into mental illness for a long time. Though I had relatives nearby, she managed to keep us fairly isolated. I felt sad and lonely most of the time.

My family experienced other close losses, and I can still feel the atmosphere of grief that blanketed our home. It was stifling and had a tinge of hopelessness to it.

I decided I wanted to go to church. I was about 10. I somehow always knew God existed, but I wanted to know more about Him. More than that, I wanted to know Him. I knew I needed to know Him if I was going to make it.

After reading some of the Bible, Jesus made sense to me. I could almost see Him in front of me - inviting me to come in His arms. I asked Him to forgive me, cleanse me, and save me.

In junior high school, a good friend died suddenly over the Christmas holidays. He sat right in front of me in homeroom. He was bright, fun, full of promise, and healthy. I began each school day staring at his empty desk.

My mom continued to decline mentally. My parents separated and divorced in my early teens. By default, I stayed with Mom. She slipped deeper and deeper into a world of grandiose delusions. She had a breakdown and was hospitalized.

I moved in with Dad. The next six months were great. Dad was stable, and his presence provided a strong sense of safety.

Then one Sunday afternoon, Dad collapsed in front of me of a massive heart attack. They were able to resuscitate his heart, but he never regained consciousness. I sat by his hospital bed, held his hand, and said everything I could possibly think of to say. I gazed at his face for long periods of time, as if I was trying to memorize it. I knew in my heart he was already gone. Once they turned off life support, he died a few hours later.

After Dad's death, Mom was even more unstable than before. She attempted to take her own life and was placed in inpatient psychiatric care.

My world, as I knew it, was over. I was 15.

A TOTAL LIFE SHIFT

In my simple teenage way, I accepted reality. Life was difficult. Bad stuff was going to happen. At the same time, all of this was more than I could handle. My anxiety and anger began to leak out. I began engaging in risky behavior. Some of my friends wondered if I had a death wish.

During all this, I knew that Jesus was there. I knew He was with me, but I honestly didn't pay much attention. I was slogging through on my own. My friends were my life at that point.

After living alone for a few months (I still don't know how that happened), one of my best friends and his dad showed up at my door. "We want you to come live with us."

I had known them for 10 years. I had been in their home numerous times. Easy decision.

From the moment I walked into their home, I felt a profound sense of safety. Even though they already had four kids, they loved, accepted, and supported me in every way imaginable. It was so good, in fact, that I simply couldn't take it all in.

One day, I asked the dad why they would take in a kid like me. He smiled and said, "Gary, with what Jesus Christ did for us, how could we not do this for you?"

I already knew Jesus, but now I was experiencing His love for me in new and profound ways through my new family. For me, it has never been about religion or churchgoing. It's always been about relationship.

I went to college and studied Psychology. Not surprisingly, my adult life has been about helping hurting people heal and grow. As I give, I heal a little bit more.

"A father to the fatherless, a defender of widows, is God in his holy dwelling. God sets the lonely in families..." (Psalm 68:5-6a).

I have experienced the truth of these words many times. Everywhere I went, God created a sense of family for me. I have been blessed indeed.

THE LOSSES KEPT COMING

As I got older, the losses continued to pile up, as they do with all of us. I lost more relatives, friends, and co-workers. With each loss, the pain of past losses came visiting and added to the grief of the present. As a missionary and pastor, I was frequently around emotional pain, grief, and loss.

Then my marriage of almost three decades ended in a divorce I did not want or agree with. The pain and confusion were intense. For the next several years, I questioned almost everything. The death of my marriage was devastating.

Amid all the pain, God was faithful. He saw me through. He empowered me as a single dad. At a time when I thought my "ministry life" was tarnished and over, He kept giving me more and more ministry. My first three books came out during this time.

When I seek God, wait, and don't try to make something happen, God surprises me. My heart warmed to an amazing lady who had lost her husband to pancreatic cancer. We dated and then married. And just after my youngest daughter graduated from high school, I inherited four more kids.

Even with all the new goodness, these last few years have been wracked with loss after loss. Life never stops - and never do the challenges and difficulties.

LIGHT IN AN UPSIDE-DOWN WORLD

And now the world itself has turned upside down. Fear, anxiety, anger, and uncertainty seem to be in the atmosphere we breathe.

Yet God has not changed. He is the steady anchor amid this storm. Jesus knows all about hardship, pain, rejection, false accusation, loneliness, separation, and death. He endured it all, bore my sins and yours, and died in our place. Death could not hold Him. He is victorious. He is life.

And He is coming back for those who have trusted Him.

If you do not yet know Him, please don't delay. He is knocking. He is calling. He is waiting for you.

He is the solution to our fears, anxieties, grief, and longings. We were created by Him and for Him.

And He is coming soon.

Amen. So be it. Come, Lord Jesus.

Are you interested in knowing what the Bible says about what's happening the world today?

Download your free pdf today:

"What in the World is Going On?"

https://www.garyroe.com/what-in-the-world

SOME BIBLE VERSES DEALING WITH FEAR

There is no fear in love. But perfect love drives out fear, because fear has to do with punishment. The one who fears is not made perfect in love.

(1 John 4:18)

"Have I not commanded you? Be strong and courageous. Do not be afraid; do not be discouraged, for the Lord your God will be with you wherever you go."

(Joshua 1:9)

The Lord is my light and my salvation— whom shall I fear? The Lord is the stronghold of my life—of whom shall I be afraid?

(Psalm 27:1)

The Lord is with me; I will not be afraid. What can mere mortals do to me?

(Psalm 118:6)

"So do not fear, for I am with you; do not be dismayed, for I am your God. I will strengthen you and help you; I will uphold you with my righteous right hand."

(Isaiah 41:10)

Overhearing what they said, Jesus told him, "Don't be afraid; just believe."

(Mark 5:36)

"Do not let your hearts be troubled. You believe in God; believe also in me. My Father's house has many rooms; if that were not so, would I have told you that I am going there to prepare a place for you? And if I go and prepare a place for you, I will come back and take you to be with me that you also may be where I am."

(John 14:1-3)

"Peace I leave with you; my peace I give you. I do not give to you as the world gives. Do not let your hearts be troubled and do not be afraid."

(John 14:27)

God is our refuge and strength,
 an ever-present help in trouble.
Therefore, we will not fear, though the earth give way
 and the mountains fall into the heart of the sea,
though its waters roar and foam
 and the mountains quake with their surging.

(Psalm 46:1-3)

"So do not fear, for I am with you; do not be dismayed, for I am your God."

(Isaiah 41:10)

"Do not be afraid, little flock, for your Father has been pleased to give you the kingdom."

(Luke 12:32)

SOME BIBLE VERSES DEALING WITH ANXIETY

He says, "Be still, and know that I am God;
I will be exalted among the nations,
I will be exalted in the earth."

(Psalm 46:10)

Search me, God, and know my heart;
 test me and know my anxious thoughts.
See if there is any offensive way in me,
 and lead me in the way everlasting.

(Psalm 139:23-24)

"I have told you these things, so that in me you may have peace. In this world you will have trouble. But take heart! I have overcome the world."

(John 16:33)

Do not be anxious about anything, but in every situation, by prayer and petition, with thanksgiving, present your requests to God. And the peace of God, which transcends all understanding, will guard your hearts and your minds in Christ Jesus.

(Philippians 4:6-7)

Humble yourselves, therefore, under God's mighty hand, that he may lift you up in due time. Cast all your anxiety on him because he cares for you.

(1 Peter 5:6-7)

SOME BIBLE VERSES DEALING WITH GRIEF

My eyes have grown dim with grief;
my whole frame is but a shadow.

(Job 17:7)

But you, God, see the trouble of the afflicted; you consider their grief and take it in hand. The victims commit themselves to you; you are the helper of the fatherless.

(Psalm 10:14)

Be merciful to me, Lord, for I am in distress; my eyes grow weak with sorrow, my soul and body with grief.

(Psalm 31:9)

The Lord is close to the brokenhearted. He saves those who are crushed in spirit.

(Psalm 34:18)

My eyes are dim with grief. I call to you, Lord, every day; I spread out my hands to you.

(Psalm 88:9)

Though He brings grief, He will show compassion,
so great is His unfailing love.
For He does not willingly bring affliction
or grief to anyone.

(Lamentations 3:32-33)

When they came together in Galilee, Jesus said to them, "The Son of Man is going to be delivered into the hands of men. They will kill him, and on the third day he will be raised to life." And the disciples were filled with grief.

(Matthew 17:22-23)

"Very truly I tell you, you will weep and mourn while the world rejoices. You will grieve, but your grief will turn to joy."

(John 16:20)

Praise be to the God and Father of our Lord Jesus Christ, the Father of compassion and the God of all comfort, who comforts us in all our troubles, so that we can comfort those in any trouble with the comfort we ourselves receive from God.

(2 Corinthians 1:3-4)

Praise be to the God and Father of our Lord Jesus Christ! In his great mercy he has given us new birth into a living hope through the resurrection of Jesus Christ from the dead, and into an inheritance that can never perish, spoil or fade. This inheritance is kept in heaven for you, who through faith are shielded by God's power until the coming of the salvation that is ready to be revealed in the last time.

In all this you greatly rejoice, though now for a little while you may have had to suffer grief in all kinds of trials. These have come so that the proven genuineness of your faith—of greater worth than gold, which perishes even though refined by fire—may result in praise, glory and honor when Jesus Christ is revealed.

Though you have not seen him, you love him; and even though you do not see him now, you believe in him and are filled with an inexpressible and glorious joy, for you are receiving the end result of your faith, the salvation of your souls.

(1 Peter 1:3-9)

SOME BIBLE VERSES ABOUT JESUS AS GOD

When Jesus saw their faith, he said to the paralyzed man, "Son, your sins are forgiven."

Now some teachers of the law were sitting there, thinking to themselves, "Why does this fellow talk like that? He's blaspheming! Who can forgive sins but God alone?"

Immediately Jesus knew in his spirit that this was what they were thinking in their hearts, and he said to them, "Why are you thinking these things? Which is easier: to say to this paralyzed man, 'Your sins are forgiven,' or to say, 'Get up, take your mat and walk'? But I want you to know that the Son of Man has authority on earth to forgive sins."

So he said to the man, "I tell you, get up, take your mat and go home."

He got up, took his mat and walked out in full view of them all.

This amazed everyone and they praised God, saying,

"We have never seen anything like this!"

(Mark 2:5-12)

In the beginning was the Word, and the Word was with God, and the Word was God. He was with God in the beginning. Through Him all things were made; without Him nothing was made that has been made. In Him was life, and that life was the light of all mankind. The light shines in the darkness, and the darkness has not overcome it.

The Word became flesh and made His dwelling among us. We have seen His glory, the glory of the one and only Son, who came from the Father, full of grace and truth.

(John 1:1-5, 14)

The woman said, "I know that Messiah" (called Christ) "is coming. When He comes, He will explain everything to us."

Then Jesus declared, "I, the one speaking to you—I am He."

(John 4:25-26)

In his defense Jesus said to them, "My Father is always at his work to this very day, and I too am working."

For this reason, they tried all the more to kill him; not only was he breaking the Sabbath, but he was even calling God his own Father, making himself equal with God.

(John 5:17-18)

Then Jesus declared, "I am the bread of life. Whoever comes to me will never go hungry, and whoever believes in me will never be thirsty."

(John 6:35)

When Jesus spoke again to the people, He said, "I am the light of the world. Whoever follows me will never walk in darkness, but will have the light of life."

(John 8:12)

But he continued, "You are from below; I am from above. You are of this world; I am not of this world. I told you that you would die in your sins; if you do not believe that I am he, you will indeed die in your sins."

(John 8:23-24)

"Very truly I tell you," Jesus answered, "before Abraham was born, I am!"

(John 8:58)

Therefore, Jesus said again, "Very truly I tell you, I am the gate for the sheep. All who have come before me are thieves and robbers, but the sheep have not listened to them. I am the gate; whoever enters through me will be saved. They will come in and go out and find pasture. The thief comes only to steal and kill and destroy; I have come that they may have life and have it to the full."

(John 10:7-10)

"I give them eternal life, and they shall never perish; no one will snatch them out of my hand. My Father, who has given them to me, is greater than all; no one can snatch them out of my Father's hand. I and the Father are one."

(John 10:28-30)

Jesus said to her, "I am the resurrection and the life. The one who believes in me will live, even though they die; and whoever lives by believing in me will never die. Do you believe this?"

(John 11:25-26)

Jesus answered, "I am the way and the truth and the life. No one comes to the Father except through me."

(John 14:6)

"I came from the Father and entered the world; now I am leaving the world and going back to the Father."

(John 16:28)

After Jesus said this, he looked toward heaven and prayed: "Father, the hour has come. Glorify your Son, that your Son may glorify you. For you granted him authority over all people that he might give eternal life to all those you have given him. Now this is eternal life: that they know you, the only true God, and Jesus Christ, whom you have sent."

(John 17:1-3)

Jesus said, "My kingdom is not of this world. If it were, my servants would fight to prevent my arrest by the Jewish leaders. But now my kingdom is from another place."

"You are a king, then!" said Pilate.

Jesus answered, "You say that I am a king. In fact, the reason I was born and came into the world is to testify to the truth. Everyone on the side of truth listens to me."

(John 18:36-37)

But Jesus remained silent.

The high priest said to him, "I charge you under oath by the living God: Tell us if you are the Messiah, the Son of God."

"You have said so," Jesus replied. "But I say to all of you: From now on you will see the Son of Man sitting at the right hand of the Mighty One and coming on the clouds of heaven."

(Matthew 26:63-64)

At daybreak the council of the elders of the people, both the chief priests and the teachers of the law, met together, and Jesus was led before them.

"If you are the Messiah," they said, "tell us."

Jesus answered, "If I tell you, you will not believe me, and if I asked you, you would not answer. But from now on, the Son of Man will be seated at the right hand of the mighty God."

They all asked, "Are you then the Son of God?"

He replied, "You say that I am."

(Luke 22:67-70)

The Son is the image of the invisible God, the firstborn over all creation. For in Him all things were created: things in heaven and on earth, visible and invisible, whether thrones or powers or rulers or authorities; all things have been created through Him and for Him. He is before all things, and in Him all things hold together.

(Colossians 1:15-17)

For in Christ all the fullness of the Deity lives in bodily form.

(Colossians 2:9)

We know also that the Son of God has come and has given us understanding, so that we may know Him who is true. And we are in Him who is true by being in his Son Jesus Christ. He is the true God and eternal life.

(1 John 5:20)

I am trying here to prevent anyone saying the really foolish thing that people often say about Him: "I'm ready to accept Jesus as a great moral teacher, but I don't accept his claim to be God."

That is the one thing we must not say.

A man who was merely a man and said the sort of things Jesus said would not be a great moral teacher. He would either be a lunatic—on a level with the man who says he is a poached egg—or else he would be the Devil of Hell.

You must make your choice. Either this man was, and is, the Son of God; or else a madman or something worse.

You can shut Him up for a fool, you can spit at Him and kill Him as a demon, or you can fall at His feet and call Him Lord and God. But let us not come away with any patronizing nonsense about His being a great human teacher.

He has not left that open to us. He did not intend to.
- C.S. Lewis, from *Mere Christianity*

Are you interested in knowing what the Bible says about what's happening the world today?

Download your free pdf today:
"What in the World is Going On?"
https://www.garyroe.com/what-in-the-world

ADDITIONAL RESOURCES

BOOKS

FOR ANY CLOSE LOSS

The Grief Guidebook: Common Questions, Compassionate Answers, Practical Suggestions

Grieving the Write Way Journal and Workbook

Grief Walk: Experiencing God After the Loss of a Loved One

Comfort for Grieving Hearts: Hope and Encouragement for Times of Loss

Please Be Patient, I'm Grieving: How to Care for and Support the Grieving Heart

Surviving the Holidays Without You: Navigating Grief During Special Seasons

FOR THOSE WHO HAVE LOST A SPOUSE

Widowed Walk: Experiencing God After the Loss of a Loved One

Comfort for the Grieving Spouse's Heart: Hope and Healing After Losing Your Partner

Heartbroken: Healing from the Loss of a Spouse

FOR THOSE WHO HAVE LOST A CHILD

Shattered: Surviving the Loss of a Child

Comfort for the Grieving Parent's Heart: Hope and Healing After Losing Your Child

FOR THOSE WHO HAVE LOST A PARENT

Comfort for the Grieving Adult Child's Heart: Hope and Healing After Losing Your Parent

FOR SUICIDE LOSS

Aftermath: Picking Up the Pieces After a Suicide

FOR THOSE WHO LIVE AND WORK WITH TEENS

Teen Grief: Caring for the Grieving Teenage Heart

FOR OVERCOMING ADVERSITY

Living on the Edge: How to Fight and Win the Battle for Your Heart and Mind (Adult & Teen Editions)

Difference Maker: Overcoming Adversity and Turning Pain into Purpose Every Day (Adult & Teen Editions)

FREE RESOURCES

Visit www.garyroe.com/free
for no-cost, practical resources.

CONNECT WITH GARY

Visit Gary at www.garyroe.com and connect with him on Facebook, YouTube, Twitter, LinkedIn, and Pinterest

Facebook: https://www.facebook.com/garyroeauthor

YouTube: https://www.youtube.com/channel/UClPGeRF5iYg1Y80h2B7MIqg

Twitter: https://twitter.com/GaryRoeAuthor

LinkedIn: https://www.linkedin.com/in/garyroeauthor

Pinterest: https://www.pinterest.com/garyroe79/

ABOUT THE AUTHOR

Gary's story began with a childhood of mixed messages and sexual abuse. This was followed by other losses and numerous grief experiences.

Ultimately, a painful past led Gary into a life of helping wounded people heal and grow. A former college minister, missionary in Japan, entrepreneur in Hawaii, pastor, and hospice chaplain, he now serves as a writer, speaker, grief specialist, and grief coach.

In addition to *Hope in a World Gone Mad*, Gary is the author of numerous books, including the award-winning bestsellers *The Grief Guidebook, Shattered: Surviving the Loss of a Child, Comfort for the Grieving Spouse's Heart,* and *Aftermath: Picking Up the Pieces After a Suicide.* Gary's books have won four international book awards and have been named finalists seven times. He has been featured on Dr. Laura, Belief Net, the

Christian Broadcasting Network, Wellness, Thrive Global, and other major media and has well over 800 grief-related articles in print. Recipient of the Diane Duncam Award for Excellence in Hospice Care, Gary is a popular keynote, conference, and seminar speaker at a wide variety of venues.

Gary loves being a husband and father. He has seven adopted children. He enjoys hockey, corny jokes, good puns, and colorful Hawaiian shirts. Gary and his wife Jen and family live in Texas.

Visit Gary at www.garyroe.com.

Don't forget to download your free PDF:

"What in the World is Going On?"

https://www.garyroe.com/what-in-the-world

ACKNOWLEDGEMENTS

Special thanks to my wife Jen for her constant support, encouragement, and wisdom. Thank you for partnering with me in sharing Jesus and helping grieving hearts heal and grow.

Special thanks to Kelli Levey Reynolds for her keen proofreading and editorial assistance. I appreciate you more than you know.

Thanks to my wonderful Advance Reader Team for their corrections, feedback, and input. You made this book so much better.

Thanks to Glendon Haddix of Streetlight Graphics for his artistic skill and expertise in design and formatting. Thank you for using your gifts to support and encourage others.

AN URGENT REQUEST

Dear Reader,

Others are scared, anxious, and grieving today. You can help.

How?

With a simple, heartfelt review.

Could you take a few moments and write a 1-3 sentence review of *Hope in a World Gone Mad* and leave it on the site you purchased the book from?

And if you want to help even more, you could leave the same review on the *Hope in a World Gone Mad* book page on Goodreads.

Your review counts and will help reach others who could benefit from this book. Thanks for considering this.

I read these reviews as well, and your comments and feedback assist me in producing more quality resources for hurting, grieving hearts.

Thank you!

Warmly,
Gary

www.ingramcontent.com/pod-product-compliance
Lightning Source LLC
Chambersburg PA
CBHW030151100526
44592CB00009B/228